ELENA SOBOLEVA

The Moon in the Eighth House

London 2023

Published by Hertfordshire Press Ltd © 2023
e-mail: publisher@hertfordshirepress.com
www.hertfordshirepress.com

ELENA SOBOLEVA

The Moon in the Eighth House

English

Translated by Andrey Vakhnin
Cover photo of Elena Soboleva by Daniil Pushkarev
Book design by Alexandra Rey

All rights reserved. No part of this book may be reprinted or reproduced or utilised in any form or by any electronic, mechanical, or other means, now known or hereafter invented, including photocopying and recording, or in any information storage or retrieval system, without permission in writing from the publishers.

British Library Catalogue in Publication Data
A catalogue record for this book is available from the British Library
Library of Congress in Publication Data
A catalogue record for this book has been requested

ISBN: 978-1-913356-64-4

CONTENTS

INSTEAD OF A PREFACE	5
SICKNESS	9
CHILDHOOD	21
BEHIND THE LOOKING GLASS	36
ROCK'N'ROLL	64
GAZ-21. THE OLD "VOLGA"	68
THE GOD OF KNEES	89
CRIMINAL DEN	121
THE MOON IN THE EIGHTH HOUSE	149
LIBERATION	175
REVIEWS	202

INSTEAD OF A PREFACE

The natal chart, the solar, transits… No chance of figuring it all out at once. So far, I've got the signs of the zodiac, and that is only if they're not in some astrological circles with a bunch of other different symbols. What a hypochondriac I have become! Seeing "tragic" planets in "bad" houses in my horoscope made me so sad. Should I really not be expecting anything good coming my way? Nonsense! I need pull myself together. What's with that sad attitude? Maybe for some people these "tragic" planets and "bad" houses can cause unpleasant events or even maybe crush their spirit, but definitely not me! My life would be too boring otherwise. All the "terrible" things that have happened in my life have been so vivid and impressive that I remember them with a smile on my face. And when I get to share these stories, there is no stopping me. And I always get a rapturous response from the listener who, having forgot how to breathe, is about to applaud.

THE MOON IN THE EIGHTH HOUSE

For me, it is either ecstasy or pain. I don't settle for anything in between. I am fate's absolute favourite. And whatever it has prepared or will prepare for me in the future is for the better.

My personal diary.
May 1990

THE MOON IN THE EIGHTH HOUSE

Got a little sick. My throat doesn't hurt anymore, but I'm still coughing and my voice is slightly hoarse. In a few days of sore throats, I had recovered from my recent stress. I needed those five days. I fully accepted my condition and the need of a hip joint replacement. I understand that some people might find it funny as in "Oh look! She is the one stressed! What does she know? Who cares about a joint... It's not the worst surgery people do!" Sure. Everything is relative. Still, I'm not some young naive girl, and I know real pain. I also know a lot about endoprosthetics as I had the pleasure (nothing else but the pleasure) of replacing my damaged joint with a new one, made of titanium. Now I am to do it one more time with my other leg. I wish I could travel in time! I would skip the hospital part, the surgery itself, the unbearable pain and the crutches... and be on my strong legs, with a confident gait and be healthy and beautiful again! Anyway... I'll have to live through every single moment and gain another bit of precious life experience... to take a look with my eyes open at the people around me and figure out who is who. In the end, hit the jackpot - a healthy life. The game is worth the candle!

My personal diary.
May 2013

THE MOON IN THE EIGHTH HOUSE

SICKNESS

Since *I am Fate's favourite*, the Sickness, which ruined my *joints,* is very careful and delicate with me; I would even say that the Sickness loves me. Let me try to explain. A long time ago, when I was no older than one, I got sick with a *devastating* disease. The doctors' sympathy for my parents was sincere but bitter, as they could only offer *"killer" hormone therapy and cytostatic treatment.* And even though the best and rarest outcome of such a treatment was a life in a wheelchair with *level 3 physical disability*, as the doctors predicted, the worst-case scenario was death.

A child is too young for such a horrible disease and such a *cruel* treatment. And it was the moment when my parents made the only right decision for me – they took me out from the hospital and didn't treat me at all. And a miracle happened. The Sickness backed away from me. So, the day when my mum took me away from the hospital was the day when I signed *"a non-aggression pact"* with the Sickness. I never tried to wipe it out with *any "killer"* therapy, and in return it never slowed me down as I was living a fulfilling, colourful life. Sometimes the Sickness even inspired some of it! In a way it shaped my character: it gave me courage, determination, autonomy and a strong will. In fact, I have received most of my positive traits because the Sickness. Certainly, my appearance is no exception, either. Apart from my ruined joints, the Sickness gifted me a thin bone structure; pure, snow-white aristocratic skin; quite an unusually shaped face, almost cartoonishly attractive. All of this made me quite different from the crowd.

My natal chart almost screams "complicated life". Any horoscope consists of twelve spheres of life, also known as houses. I have an overflowing house of "illness" and "death" and complex aspects of struggle in between. Over time, having become a good astrologer, I have learned to move among the planets and thus adjust my life a little bit; or maybe not a little.

But the horoscope *always manifests itself* and everything is bound to happen in our life, whatever is written in it. And if there is an indication of a severe illness, unfortunately, it cannot be avoided. Still there are some tricks! In my lifetime I have seen a lot of horoscopes of people suffering from various, very serious, sometimes even fatal illnesses. But those horoscopes often weren't as horrendous as my own. Nevertheless, those people were going through a lot of suffering, some of them even being bedridden. For them I was just the "lucky one"! That got me wondering… why is it whenever somebody achieves any success in life, even the tiniest drop of it, it is easier for people to call it luck? Although luck is a very good thing, my dear readers, it wasn't the defining factor of my life! The only source of good is Jupiter that commands our fortune, and in my natal chart Jupiter's position is far worse than just negative, so relying on luck was never a way for me. Without any shortcuts in my life, I have to fiercely fight through it on my own and definitely win! And although, honestly speaking, my horoscope says very little about "winning", I've latched onto this aspect with all the strength I have! Musculoskeletal diseases are normally associated with Saturn in astrology.

Saturn is a tragic planet. The planet of grief, deprivation and pain. Saturn's positioning in relation to other stars, personal planets is always unfortunate; and it can also be found in some houses (like that of "illnesses", "death" and "confinement") in the horoscopes of people who suffer from joint diseases. Oftentimes Saturn can be a part of some evil aspect figure that is symbolically associated with struggle. And that's exactly how it is in my own horoscope. However, being completely unaware of the astrological intricacies, peo-

THE MOON IN THE EIGHTH HOUSE

ple misuse these grave aspects of struggle trying to fight the disease itself. And mind you, their fight is endless, but it doesn't bring them any victory, so they get even worse. Eventually, the disease results in a severe form of disability. Obviously. Saturn is impossible to win against. The mere idea of that is too presumptuous. For example, in India and in some other places, the God of Saturn is highly revered and feared. The God's name in Sanskrit is Shani. And a legend has it that Ganesha, a beloved Hindu deity, lost his human head as an infant, just from one look at Shani. Can you imagine? If Saturn is capable of bashing other gods' heads, what about us, mortals? There are other ways of applying those aspects of struggle. And in fact, that's what I did. And I am in no way preaching my ways, I just want to share my experience. This book is definitely not my full autobiography.

It only contains a few stories from my life, both funny and sad. But even the funny moments, and you'll see it, are full of the struggle I wrote about earlier. Never in my entire life have I ever received anything for free, my horoscope is way too unkind in that regard. For the smallest things in life, I've had to fight with society, with circumstances, anything.

In our world I am considered an attractive and vibrant woman. When someone compliments me, I only smile back and say that I am just very lucky to have beautiful parents. But that's not completely true.

My Sickness had a hand, too. I've got a strong feeling that my Sickness has long repented for attacking me, a one-year-old, once and is now trying to atone itself keeping my body in perfect health, even though some of my joints are damaged. I don't have any regrets; my Sickness is my friend. My Sickness is my right hand. Because of it, in my life I've mostly had WONDERFUL men. Ever since I was fifteen and up until now, I've had a solid reputation of a girl who always gets the best Men.

THE MOON IN THE EIGHTH HOUSE

I first started exploring astrology in my childhood, and back then I already knew that our Universe is no joke, and that "freedom of choice" which is promised to us by birth is nothing but a collective illusion. In reality we can only "move" solely within the framework of the planets since we all live in the same Solar system and by the same rules. Our Solar system is infested with evildoers such as Mars, Saturn, Uranus, Neptune, Pluto. All of these planets are anything but kind or good to us. So, over the course of their lives, people have to adapt somehow – getting hurt, experiencing unfairness, destitution, illnesses, death of relatives and friends… You see, people have to deal with numerous misfortunes and troubles. And still, our Universe is beautiful!

And with the knowledge of its grand plans, we can make our life truly happier! The very same Saturn negatively positioned in the horoscope, commanding joint diseases offers no definite diagnosis! And joints can hurt very differently. They can hurt without causing any harm to a person's quality of life or they can lead to a wheelchair. Nonetheless, in both cases, Saturn will be in an equally unfortunate position. And there are definitely going to be aspects of struggle. And most of the time, these are the aspects that decide the fate of the joints. In other words, it is very important how the person fights. And what the person fights. There is bound to be a lot of fighting. That's what I do all my life. But not against my Sickness!

We all know or we've heard at least once about the founding law of the Universe – the law of least resistance. All events in our lives happen in the most logical, and therefore the easiest way. That's why when I work with my clients, and just by looking at their horoscope right away I tell them all the truth about them, they are sometimes very surprised!! Is it really so clearly written? Of course! Because that important law is in action here. The Universe has no reason to bother and make up extraordinary stories for us; it's much easier to make life predictable. And this is where that "freedom of choice" appears and the person gets a chance of changing their fate.

The planets in the sky set the trends for us. And in according to these trends, we "move". For example, that tragic Saturn, ill-positioned in the house of "Illness", doesn't care at all what negative events happen to our bones and joints. One thing is certain: they will happen, no doubt. And if we follow the law of least resistance, then obviously, given this trend, the person goes to the hospital and begins to fight the disease. Because it makes sense. And this is the natural order of events. But you and I remember that this is a trend of NEGATIVE events! Which means, eventually it'll end up bad. The only good thing about this situation is that the aspect of struggle is of a "non-permanent" nature, hitting a person from time to time. In medicine, they call it periods of disease exacerbation and remission. I have always acted irrationally. I try my best not to follow the Great Law of the Universe. I have a rebellious spirit inside me! If I loosen up and follow it, I will definitely end up in a wheelchair. And that is not the most unpleasant thing I have seen in my horoscope. But the trend still stands and we are only allowed to "move" within the trend, so almost all the events in my life touch upon the subject of "illness" and "joints" in one way or another. And I get a portion of negative events, as was promised by the Universe, and serious ones, too! But they don't result in severe disability, but always in something else.

For more than twenty years, women and men of all ages and social statuses have been asking me for advice and astrological consultations. Girls always ask how to find a worthy man, who to get married with, how to make anyone fall in love with them, how to improve relations with their current partner, how to lose weight, how to become more charming, and so on. I am very glad that thanks to my knowledge and an alternative view on life, I can be useful to people. During my short life so far, I have known a huge number of people of both sexes, I have figured out their problems, I have learned their psychology. For a long time now, it's been quite easy for me to understand almost any human problem, to understand where the problem "grows" from and to help people to get rid of their insecurities. It is obvious that any so-called "defect" can be turned into the biggest advantage. And this advantage will become a trap for good luck in life. For example, I remember my surgeon, a wonderful doctor, seeing me after rehabilitation for the replacement of the first hip joint; I was happy, easily walking in high heels, and he told me, "Don't tell anybody that you have an artificial joint, no one will know, except for you." Know what? Know that I have a disease and need serious surgery like this? It's a good breeding ground for inferiority complexes. No way! I told him back then that if I could, I would walk on my ass, to show the whole world how good it is!

In fact, I wanted to put a sign on myself saying: "I DID IT!". My buttock alone is worth $10,000, imagine how expensive I am as a whole woman! How can I keep quiet about that?! My titanium joint became such a HUGE lure for men that I was just drowning in men's attention, compliments and love! It was only when I was far and deep in my childhood that I was insecure about my Disease, not knowing how to respond to questions from people who wondered why I was a little different from others. I used to get upset and wanted to be like everyone else. But years later I took a closer look at "everyone else" I had tried so hard to be like as a child. "Everyone else" turned out to be very dysfunctional people, with a difficult fate; with huge, clear insecurities, bad taste, poor education and upbringing. And all those people, mostly even adults, not their children, tried to point out my "inferiority". Only since I was fifteen years old, have I stopped meeting those "gifted" people; somehow, they just quietly walked out of my life line.

Although I remember a few years ago, before my first surgery, when I was moving with great difficulty and pain, a hairdresser was giving me a haircut. He cut my hair perfectly, the color of my hair was perfect too, and my reflection in the mirror smiled at me.

And that's when a woman like "everyone else" showed up. I don't know what brought her into my life line, but it was even kind of funny at the time. The woman looked thoroughly exhausted: unkempt, with badly done makeup and a lot of extra pounds.

Stopping beside satisfied and radiant me, she raised her hand, pointing to my attractive reflection in the mirror and said,

So why do you need all this? Why show off? You can't walk anyway!

And I broke out in a smile. It had been a long time since I'd heard such nonsense!

Yes, I can't walk. But I can sit all pretty like this! And you, unfortunately, can neither sit pretty nor walk pretty.

It's been years since that incident. People with life lines that I can't understand don't come around me anymore. Perhaps that woman must have told "everyone else" that I didn't care anymore and it's no use asserting dominance at my expense.

I called Mr M. He is the surgeon. But not the same one from the last time. Last time it was Mr G. Mr G. is a two-meter tall, broad-shouldered, stately man with noble gray hair and a quiet voice. The first time we met, he made a good impression on me, which I obviously was not expecting from a doctor. Well, somehow my relationship with doctors did not work out too well at that time.

When I, full of excitement, with a lot of interjections and occasional swear words, waving my arms widely, was telling him my horrible(!) story and was trying to give him

advice on how I should be operated, he listened to me with a calm half-smile, like the Mona Lisa, and at the end of my fiery speech in a very simple way he said,

— Don't worry about it, you'll be fine.

And everything was fine. Very good even. After rehabilitation, I soared! I was over the moon! What a bliss it was to be thin, beautiful, and healthy! Of course, I knew that I would have to change the other joint as well, but I did not want to think about it. I enjoyed every moment of my healthy life, living right here and right now!

That's it... The time has come... It's time again. This time Mr. G. will operate on me at the clinic where Mr M. works and so, they work together. The Internet is flooded with positive and not so positive reviews about Mr. M. In some reviews people only wanted him to operate on them. Others say that he is the best. Others say he is too great and impossible to get to. And others curse him...well, as usual. It's the Internet. I have already met Mr. M. He is an elderly but incredibly energetic, emotional and very talkative man. He has prepared a long list of doctors that I have to go to and the tests that I have to take before hospitalization. So... good luck to me!

My personal diary
May 2013

CHILDHOOD

I have never been officially diagnosed with disability. I did not and do not consider it necessary for me. But generally, I could always get the diagnosis. And there's even metalwork in my body already. And so, I am a differently abled person. But what is "differently abled"? Probably everyone has their own understanding of this phrase. As for me, my "abilities" to wash dishes, to cook, to handwash clothes or to go grocery shopping or to do anything that I do not enjoy are definitely "different" as I've excluded them from my life... All that which I don't enjoy, I have crossed out of my life. It's my right to do so since I am "differently abled"! The only things I have left in my life are the things that I enjoy, namely my hobbies: my favorite astrology, psychology, fashion and beauty, music, books, entertainment, and of course, um... men! My Men are the greatest accomplishment of my life! From communicating with me, they have learned everything: how to cook delicious food, how to conduct business competently and earn good money, what kind of gifts

I prefer and how to take better care of me. I hope my beloved men won't hate me for such presumptuous statements! For more than twenty years I have been surrounded only by Real Men, who know how to deal with any problem, allowing me to enjoy life and not to worry about anything. And life is good!

You, my dear readers, might ask me where I found such amazing men. It's simple. A long time ago, in my youth, I decided that I deserved to have only the best men, whose heads I would turn and whom I would inspire to heroic deeds. I decided to become exactly the kind of Woman, whom no man I needed could ever resist. My transformation into a femme fatale began with a sober examination of myself from head to toe in a large mirror. The mirror clearly laughed at me and gave me an impressively awful reflection. My head was of an irregular geometric shape, with an overly large, disproportionate forehead and a small chin, attached to my torso by a thin, long neck. The body was flat, thin, and angular, without any hint of femininity, with arms and legs deformed by the sickness. The deathly pale girl in the mirror smiled: "Well, all right … So be it. It's all right. It's beautiful. We'll just introduce new standards of beauty".

THE MOON IN THE EIGHTH HOUSE

No sooner said than done. From that moment on, I presented myself as a very slender and trim girl with a gorgeous thin waist at 57 centimeters, with a great figure, without a hint of "fat", with aristocratic white skin, a swan neck and high forehead, which, in turn, was an obvious indicator of my great mind, wisdom and knowledge of life. As for my deformed joints, they added mystery, a myth to my image... "A girl with a complicated fate" ... or "A girl who has been through a lot" ... or "A girl with enormous willpower" ... I learned the ropes of correct and fashionable makeup, got myself a beautiful hairdo, became an embodiment of "an incredibly attractive girl with a very interesting and complicated fate," and... people reached out to me like bees to honey! They became interested in my life, started asking what music I listen to, what books I read, what brand of cosmetics I use; they copied me, my style; they started diets to be as slender. And believe me, all that is just me being humble and modest! And so, for many years I grew more and more new legends about myself, most of which, I must admit, flattered my self-esteem. Of course, after such a high estimate, which I initially gave myself, and which then all the people around me picked up, thus strengthening my self-confidence, I used the right to personally choose Men for myself. For those Men whom I chose as my life partner, the very idea of being with an "incredibly attractive girl with a very interesting and complicated fate" was fascinating. My Men had never been with such an unusual girl before, so they behaved very differently with me than they did with others. But it wasn't always like that. For the first fourteen years of my life, I was very lonely and miserable. I can't even remember now if there was a single person among the ones who knew me at those awful times who didn't point out my inferiority. Parents often forbade their children to be friends or play with me, probably thinking that my sickness could be contagious. I remember my school teacher, loudly reprimanding me to the whole class,

— Soboleva! You're holding your pen wrong! Fix it right this minute and hold it like others!

I was very embarrassed of my deformed joints, so I answered quietly, almost whispering,

— I can't. My fingers hurt...

But she wouldn't let up,

— Then what are you doing in a school for normal and healthy children? Go to a different school, one for the sick and retarded!

And the whole class burst out laughing...

I choked back tears, I felt ashamed of myself; of my hideous, stiff joints; of just me being ugly. And during breaks between the lessons, the children would often bully and beat me. Sometimes they intentionally "set me up" in front of the teachers to make fun of me later, saying that I had done something terrible which I obviously didn't do. And then, with great agitation and devilish gleam in her eyes, the teacher would call me to the chalkboard and instead of the lesson she'd insult me in front of my classmates, until the bell rang, always pointing out my inferiority. There was no point justifying myself, not that I tried to. The boys and girls at school kept coming up with more and more ways of making fun of me, and in the end, on the day when all the children were accepted as pioneers, I was simply not accepted... It came as a complete surprise to me, because I was anxiously awaiting that very day! I had bought and ironed a pioneer necktie, put on my dress uniform with a white apron, and learned the solemn promise by heart. But it turned out that for a few days, the whole school already knew that I would not be accepted as a pioneer with all the others at the ceremonial parade, and from me it was carefully hidden. Both adults and children had come up with a new pastime. The reason behind my cruel disgrace at the parade was the old nickname of our homeroom teacher, *"Dried Roach [1]", which, of course, was allegedly invented and spread by me all around the school and beyond its walls.*

---

1   *a European freshwater fish*

THE MOON IN THE EIGHTH HOUSE

But I really did call her that. Everyone did. Moreover, when I first came to that school, on the very first day, the other students told me about her nickname. I agree, it's not nice, and I don't know about now, but in my childhood, students often gave their teachers nicknames. Our homeroom teacher was not spared that fate. Apparently, someone had given her this nickname because she was too thin. The teacher was bitter toward the world, tall, hunched over, and very thin. She also hated children. This Dried Roach used to call her students "stumps with eyes", and during the lessons she often lost control and hit the children with her pointer wherever she could. But not all of them, of course! She had her favorites, and with them she was pure as the driven snow. Already then it seemed to me something shameful and awkward for a grown-up to ingratiate and "cajole" so much a favourite student in front of the entire class, who not only did not learn the lesson and was late, but also whose behaviour was plainly unacceptable. But for some reason our head teacher preferred not to notice it in such children. Her favourites were untouchable. And you had to keep away from them as far as possible, because these children, well aware of their entitled status, were not afraid to use it every day. More often than not, it was because of them that I got my ass kicked by Dried Roach. Her favorites said nasty things and gossiped about me. And the teacher would grab her heart theatrically, shriek at the whole class, insult me, and hit me with her pointer.

In our school, the teachers were rarely called by their name and patronymic. *Dried Roach* knew about her unflattering nickname and, of course, tried to fight it, but it was all in vain. The whole school, including the teachers and even the headteacher, still called her that. The associations were probably too strong. More often than from the others, I heard this "Dried Roach" nickname from my gym teacher, who never hesitated to ask some student to bring her the class roll. Mind you, having the children lined up in front of her, she would ask loud and clear (not to mention the gymnasium's great acoustics) her regular question,

— Well? Who's going to *Dried Roach* to get the roll today?

I don't think she even knew what our head teacher's real name was. The children always giggled happily when they heard the teachers' nicknames from the adults' mouths. It showed the adults' approval! So, the kids were doing everything right!

The whole school and almost all the parents of the students gathered at the ceremony. This time I was shamed in front of the whole crowd, and the newly minted pioneers, the young Leninists, were giggling happily. This was a very important step in my life. I didn't shed a single tear; I wasn't even hurt. My childhood was irrevocably over. The whole show seemed to me to be a ridiculous and talentless theatre with very bad actors. It was a pure farce, and very badly performed. All their high-flown speeches about how a nobody like me was not worthy of wearing a tie along with the honest and diligent young Leninists; about how in the old days they would not have been so ceremonious with me, and they would have just put me against the wall and shot me; about how the whole school was weeping that such a horrible person as me was studying there, were completely unrealistically far-fetched. The funny thing was that EVERYONE, absolutely EVERYONE - teachers and students alike - knew that they were all just as guilty as I was! It was a game where everyone got their roles in advance, learned the script, even rehearsed for a few days... And probably there were people who had to go against their will and didn't want to play this cruel game, but were told to. I remember, for example, the eyes of the very gym teacher who used this nickname more often than the others, but, of course, she did not stand up for me, as she was standing at the ceremony and was trying to look down at her feet so as not to cross her eyes with mine, playing the role of a dumb extra, as ordered.

I remember a few other faces in the crowd, clearly bored and not enjoying the mayhem that much. There were only a few of them, but they still submitted to the opinion of the majority anyway. Can you imagine their life after that? Their lives, the lives of adults - I'm not even taking silly schoolchildren, who staged such a grandiose spectacle only to make fun of a small child with health issues, into account now!

At that time, the school was obliged to accept all children of fitting age, so the very next day after school, my teacher called me and said quietly,

— Okay, Soboleva, we forgive you. You can put on a tie.

My childhood was over. Somehow, very quickly, in that one day, I had become a lot older. I looked at my head teacher impassively,

— I don't need your tie; I don't want to be a pioneer anymore!

— Who cares what you want?! You have to! Put it on! - The teacher yelled at me.

— I don't want to and I won't, - I said calmly, indifferently, and even with a smirk.

— How dare you?! Who let you talk to me like that, you little shit?! Put your tie on immediately, like I said! Or I'm taking you to the principal! - the teacher yelled at me and grabbed her pointer.

— Well, let's go! I have something to tell him! And put away your pointer! I'm not afraid of you! I'll tell the principal that you beat my sore thumbs! How you insult me all the time, how you lower my grades and how you planned that whole yesterday's spectacle! You know perfectly well that the whole school calls you that nickname! Let's go! Well, why aren't you coming? Get up! Do you have any idea how much I know about you?!

Now it was me shouting and bluffing, and of course I knew nothing about her, except that she was a mediocre teacher and a complete idiot. But I was probably bluffing so convincingly that the teacher quickly grabbed my arms and sat me down next to her in a chair,

— Hush, hush... Keep your voice down! Calm down, please... We're not going to the principal... Please, just put on the tie and that's it... There won't be any problems...

— There won't be any problems for who? - I spoke in a snide and very mature way.

— For you and for me...

— Well, I don't have any problems, - I sharply interrupted the teacher.

— All right, all right. There won't be any problems for me...The principal told me that everyone in my class must wear ties... Of course, you were accepted as a pioneer, we just had to do this... and by the way, it wasn't my idea to begin with. So, it wasn't my fault. It was the PTA's suggestion that perhaps you should not be accepted... Well, who else? The rest of the kids are all normal, and you ... Plus, the other children do not like you, and we agreed ... The parents of the students begged us ... And the principal also knew everything. So, I'm not sure what you want to tell him...

The teacher's revelations were overwhelming. Of course, I knew that at the time I was an outcast, and that both adults and children could not stand me, but I couldn't even imagine the full extent of such human hatred toward myself, a small and not quite healthy child. Even the parents of students at the school, whom I had never seen before, tried to drive me out and make fun of me!

— You just need to go to another school. There are schools for the sick... Or homeschooling... right now you're among the normal kids... of course no one likes it! Neither the children nor their parents. Parents come up to me all the time, asking me to take you away from the normal kids!

— Normal?! - I shrieked. My heart was pounding and my voice was shaking. – You're all sick in the head! You have no idea how sick you are! Enough, I have

THE MOON IN THE EIGHTH HOUSE

nothing more to talk to you about!

The teacher tried to say something more, to ask me to wear a tie again, but I silently walked out of the classroom without turning around. At a bus stop, I got on a trolleybus and without a destination I rode around in circles, looking out the window, deeply absorbed in my new adult life.

After a few hours of riding, the woman driver, announcing the stops, turned to me and said very rudely and believably that she had long noticed me in the trolleybus and that if I did not get off at the nearest stop, she would turn me in to the police as a vagrant. I got off. I did put the tie on, though. In front of my apartment door, so as not to upset my mum. I almost stopped going to school altogether. My teacher didn't mind, it made her feel better. She drew C's and sometimes B's in my report card, as if I had attended classes. I lied to my parents telling them "what we studied today" and "what we had to do at home". I used to write my own marks in my gradebook, mostly A's, copying the teacher's signature. Instead of school, I would go for rides around the city, exploring its sights, and I even went to nearby towns, exploring the area there as well. In those days there were often vigilantes walking the streets, catching drunks and hooligans.

Sometimes they happened to catch me, a small child with a schoolbag. The vigilantes would ask me where I lived, why I wasn't in school, why I was alone and where my parents were... Several times they tried to take me to the police station, but somehow, I always managed to answer all their questions so well that they always let me go. I cleverly learned to make up any stories right on the spot. My voice began to sound convincing and very mature.

Then our family moved to another city. It was a big city, the capital of one of the republics of the former Soviet Union.

I spent my teenage years there, and that, actually, was the worst time, which no snotty pioneers could compare to. And during the last year I lived there, I completely turned my life upside down. I put everything on the line. I had nothing to lose, because becoming a bigger outcast that I was at that time was just impossible. Daily bullying and insults, making fun of me and beatings - it couldn't go on like that. Teenagers and their dull-witted parents turned out to be far more inventive than those little pioneers and teachers I wrote about before; it was to the point that every day of my horrible life was already unbearable. So, I changed my attitude to myself. I titled myself the

BEST. And not just the BEST, but the One and Only who could not be copied. I made everyone believe it! My transformation was almost immediate, because of my "fourteen years at the school of life". Already at the age of fifteen, I was in unprecedented demand and popular. I was offered movie roles, and modeling agencies vied with each other to recruit me. In tenth grade, I was already studying theatre at a university, and at the music school in piano class I was immediately enrolled in sixth grade! I wasn't even trying to achieve something on purpose - all the doors opened in front of me on their own. And life became fabulous. I had crowds of admirers, ready to do "anything" for me in their youthful maximalism. I literally took this city by the throat and held it tightly, not letting it go. I abolished my school uniform and went to class exclusively in full makeup. In those days it was not allowed. But I wanted to. I rarely went to school, preferring it to the theatre classes at university or just fun trips with my buddies. This time my teachers gave me good marks for my numerous absences. So, I ended up with an almost perfect diploma and a huge life experience.

BEHIND THE LOOKING GLASS

I wrote about my joyless and difficult childhood, and it thought occurred to me that if we're crying over our insecurities, then we are bound to encounter people who will laugh at us and add some extra things to cry over. If they hit you and you fall, then they will keep on hitting for the rest of our lives, until we firmly and loudly say "That's it!" And probably people can't be either "bad" or "good," it all depends on how we allow or don't allow them to treat us. I call that childhood life of mine the Looking Glass. Behind the looking glass, everything is ugly and distorted beyond recognition: the people, their actions and words, all the events. Looking-glass is the very bottom, the lowest circle of hell of a sort, and if, by accident, you find yourself here, you have to get yourself out by hook or by crook, no matter how difficult it may seem. The looking-glass sucks you in. There is no joy and happiness, no peace of mind here, only a vision of complete hopelessness, melancholy and despair. But you can get out of anything. Even from the looking glass. After my triumphant exit from that hell, fate repeatedly tried to throw me back, as if playing a test: could I stand it or not? Sometimes I made silly mistakes, getting too close to the looking-glass, but I managed to fix them with lightning speed and to hold on to my beautiful life line. And so it was, until one rainy day I found myself there again...

It happened a few years ago when I felt a pang of severe pain in my left hip joint. Since the society of "healthy" people had long ago accepted me into its ranks, and

I had felt physically well for more than twenty years, I had completely forgotten that the Sickness that had attacked me at the age of one was not sore throat, chicken pox or some kind of rash, but a severe autoimmune disease of the connective tissue and that the consequences of its attack could be extremely unpleasant. At first, I thought it would "pass on its own", then, since "it didn't pass on its own", I started taking high doses of painkillers and rubbing various ointments on the joint. My man massaged me every day, but that hardly helped either. My physical and mental condition was getting worse every day. I noticed with horror that my left leg was somehow shorter than my right leg, and my whole body was curved to one side. My gait left a lot to be desired. Passers-by began to look at me and whisper behind my back, and I began to feel embarrassed to walk in front of people. And that was the first sign of being behind the Looking Glass! The unbearable pains were growing, and I decided to go to a medical institution that had a similar name with my illness. I deliberately will not write the name of the hospital, as I do not want to offend the GOOD doctors, who certainly work there. The thing is that we couldn't cross paths with them behind the Looking Glass where I had already been trapped. I came to this medical institution. I knew nothing about my illness at the time. That is, nothing at all. I only knew that I fell ill with it when I was one year old and that I had never been treated for it, but there was a record of the time when I was diagnosed with this terrible disease, and it was already in the last, fourth stage. Until that moment my Sickness hadn't really bothered me for many years. The ruined joints were not a problem for me, and I did not pay any mind to them at all. That's all right if they were too bendy. In more than twenty years, I had never met anyone with a similar condition. I had no idea that this diagnosis usually resulted in a first type disability, and in its harshest form. I have never had a disability, and I have never gone to a doctor, except for the only time when my mother took me out of the hospital when I was very young and did not allow me to be treated with the "killer" therapy. So, at the time I went to the doctors I had no idea about the severity of my illness. I was sure that they would just give me some magic pill, I would feel better, and I would go home quietly. But there is no such thing behind the Looking Glass.

It was explained to me that before the doctor would talk to me, I had to take a detailed blood test and X-rays of all my joints. I obediently did all this and went to the hospital. The doctor's office who I had an appointment with was on the top floor, and slowly, through the pain I waddled to the elevator. There were two doctors standing by the elevator, talking about something. When they saw me, they stopped talking and looked with contempt (pure contempt!) at how I was barely able to move. One of them said:

— What are you doing here?! Take the stairs! The elevator is for doctors only! My pain was so severe that I was close to fainting at the mere thought of walking up the stairs.

— Are you kidding me? I can't take the stairs! I can't walk!

— Well, you've got two of your feet, so, you can walk after all! - The second doctor argued, - Take the stairs!

THE MOON IN THE EIGHTH HOUSE

The doors of the elevator opened, the doctors got in, and left me standing outside. The elevator left. The pain, the mockery from the doctors, and the despair made me want to scream at the whole hospital, but that time I still managed to get to the top floor in another elevator that came up just in time. As it turned out later, I wasn't the only one the doctors made such a cruel joke on. Really, they did not let poor people with musculoskeletal diseases in the elevators. And these poor people, some on crutches, some with canes, breathing heavily and barely moving, had to climb up the stairs. At the same time, the privileged and healthy doctors used the elevators freely. Now that I am writing about it, and think: HOW can this be possible? What kind of a cruel joke is this? It's just nonsense! But, believe me, it was so, and the next time behind this looking-glass, I found myself on the stairs among others like me. Just like everyone else, I was climbing up and sobbing in pain.

A red-haired woman, wearing big glasses, with an unpleasant tone of voice, a female doctor, M.D., looking at my X-rays, shook her head and said,

— Uh-oh! That's awful! How do you live with that?

— What's wrong with it? - I wondered, because I noticed that she was looking at an X-ray of my hands, and my hands didn't hurt at all. Moreover, I was driving a car without power steering at the time, so my fingers were tenacious, my grip was strong, and my muscles were pumped up.

— It's really bad. I would say really bad. You say, you've been sick for more than twenty years? Well, yes, it's evident... Did you know that people with your disease don't live that long?

— Well, I'm alive! - To say that I was shocked is not to say anything!

— Well, it's not for long... - The doctor continued, examining my scans. – I don't quite understand what you want from me? Why did you come? You should have begun treatment before, now it's too late, nothing can help you - she put the scans aside and took my test results:

— Yes, your blood tests say you're almost on the deathbed! At least you will die young! - The doctor was clearly enjoying her words.

— I'm not going to die, what are you talking about? My hip hurts. Maybe you could tell me how to treat it?

The doctor laughed viciously,

— Treat?! You should have received treatment before! You're more than twenty years too late for treatment! Are you completely brainless?! And where were your parents? What kind of parents are they? Did they not care so much about their child? That's it! It's too late! Nothing can help you anymore! This is the first time I've ever seen something like this! You are dying and have never received any sort of treatment?! Do you know what your sed rate is? And C-reactive protein?

The doctor shouted and used medical terms that I didn't understand. I didn't understand anything she was saying at all at the time. All I felt was pain in my hip. I came for medical attention and expected to get it, and, of course, I had no idea that I was already dying. I was young, and I really wanted to live!

— No! It's awful! - wailed the doctor. – How could you bring yourself to such a state?! What were you thinking?! Go to your parents and tell them it's their fault you're dying! Maybe they will, at least, feel some shame! Okay, tough luck with the parents, but yourself? You're an adult now! You could have gone to the hospital to get registered!

The doctor had gone off the deep end. Her eyes glistened, in her fiery speech she switched to the first-name basis with me,

— Okay, I'll try to do something for you, put you in the hospital. But no promises! I'm warning you right away: we're going to give you a base, we're going to give you hormones, maybe you'll get better... prepare

THE MOON IN THE EIGHTH HOUSE

yourself! You're going to be in the hospital for a long time. And remember, I'm doing you a huge favor. No one's going to take care of you now. You're dying. You should thank your parents for that. If they'd treated you since you were a kid, you'd still be alive... maybe...

I remember somehow trying to justify myself to her, to justify my parents... As if it didn't hurt, we did not know that it was so serious... But the doctor never let me finish a single sentence. Thoroughly excited, widely gesticulating, she convinced me that in my case everything was extremely neglected, that I had just a couple of months to live, that no one would ever undertake my treatment, and that only she, my savior, would try to help me, although she does not guarantee the success of the treatment, because all my joints needed to be replaced by artificial ones, and with such terrible blood tests and such terrible bones as mine it was unreal, no surgeon would do it.

Looking ahead, I would like to say that nevertheless, the doctor did me a favor. Thanks to this difficult conversation with her, I learned about joint replacement surgeries. Before, of course, I had never even heard of such a miracle.

Out of fear and total confusion I agreed to be admitted to the hospital. In incomprehensible handwriting, on medical forms the doctor began to describe "my medical record", as it turned out later, she had invented it by herself. That is, she began to write down all those symptoms of the disease which I had never had, but which, as she thought, should certainly be. Her writing really fit the description of a terminally ill person, but at that time I was so shocked by what I had heard about myself that I paid no attention to it.

I cried bitterly for days on end. I felt endless pity for myself, for my youth and beauty. In my despair and tears, I lamented about the greatest injustice in the world. Why was it happening to me? Why me? My whole life was flashing before my eyes, and I savored every pleasant memory of it, trying to relive it, at least in my mind. The man I was living with at the time was truly a saint. He worshipped me in the literal sense of the word and was ready to go through all the trials that befell me. And, he never got discouraged, always found the right words to comfort me, and believed in luck like no one else. He was always there for me. In the hardest and most difficult moments of my life. When I could not walk, he carried me in his arms, and he did it easily and with pleasure. He took complete care of me when I was completely bedridden, and he did it with some jokes and humor, always in a cheerful mood so that I did not feel any embarrassment. Then he taught me to walk on crutches, and it was also funny when he imitated women's runway walk, because that was the gait I wanted to learn! My man replaced everyone else in my life. He became my mom and dad, my husband and lover, and my best friend all in one. Largely thanks to his positive constant and powerful support I eventually broke out of the Looking Glass.

But it was still a long way off. I was admitted to the hospital. With my spirits completely down, almost dead inside and in anticipation of physical death, as I had been promised, I climbed the stairs, overcoming the intense pain, to the top floor to the doctor's office. The doctor, filling out the "Patient Card" (to be honest, I do not remember what this document is called exactly), assigned me to a hospital room. The room was on another floor and, as usual, I had only the stairs to myself again. People in white coats, as if on purpose, were patrolling at the elevator and did not allow the patients to enter it.

There were five other people in the room besides me, four of whom had the same disease as I did, and one woman with another disease, but also a very severe autoimmune disease. I sat down on my bed and observed the surroundings. The woman on the right was lying and groaning. Her primary care physician came to see her.

— Is it bad? - he asked the woman.

— Very bad. Everything hurts. Can I have a pill? - The woman groaned, and tears came out of her eyes.

— No! We had a deal! Be patient! - The doctor said it firmly.

— It really hurts, - the woman sobbed. – I can't take it anymore...

— Be patient! - The doctor said as he left the room.

The woman started crying. The other patients looked at her sympathetically, someone even encouraged her: come on...

I felt insanely sorry for her, her attending physician spoke to her somewhat sternly and indifferently. I went up to the woman and asked,

— Is there anything I can do for you? I have some ibuprofen with me, can I give it to you? It's not much of a pain reliever, of course, but it's better than nothing.

— Thank you, - replied the poor woman. – I can't. The doctor won't let me. He's writing some kind of dissertation, and he needs to know how long I can tolerate the pain without anesthesia...

— Wow, - I was very surprised. The lengths people would go for money. – Excuse me for being so straightforward, but how much do they pay you for this?

It was probably the funniest joke of that day the patients had heard. They all laughed, and even the woman who was in great pain and was crying a minute before cheered up and smiled.

— Where did you come from? the Moon? Nobody pays me anything.

— We're the only ones paying here, - the woman at the window picked up on it. - In order to get an injection or an IV from the nurse, for two different prices. And the attending doctor is a different topic. I had to borrow so much money to come here... because no one does anything for free, they won't even come close to you. Wait, did you come here without money?

— I... have money... I just don't understand then, what's the point of you tolerating this pain? – I turned again to the woman who didn't get a pill.

— Let me give you ibuprofen... if the doctor wants to experiment on you, then he should pay you money for it! What are you suffering for?

The woman perked up.

— Okay! But everyone, keep quiet! Remember, you saw nothing!

— Don't fret, we don't give up on our own! Drink, and stop the suffering! - the other patients supported the woman.

The woman took her pills, and I sat back down on my bed and continued observing. A nurse came in. She administered IVs to two women, one of whom had a different diagnosis than the rest of us, and left. About twenty minutes later she came back into the room and, with a silly laugh, she slapped her palm against her forehead:

— I just realized it now! I got your IVs mixed up!

The nurse rearranged the half-empty IVs and murmured on her way out of the room:

— Well, why didn't you say anything, you cows? Didn't you see what you were getting? It's your own fault!

To my great surprise, the "cows" began to muttering under their breath:

— Oh, I didn't notice... - said one.

— I didn't pay attention either... We're fools, you and me both... - replied another one. – It's our own fault! And now we got the wrong medicine.

I was indignant to no end!

— It wasn't your fault at all! Only the nurse is to blame! How can you stand for such attitude? They gave you the wrong medicine! You should definitely complain to the doctor!

— You are definitely not from this planet! Is this your first time in hospital? Don't you know the rules? - The woman with the IV spoke to me like I was an idiot. – The nursing staff is untouchable! The only one to blame is the patient!

I tried to argue, but when I remembered how I climbed the stairs to the sixth floor in great pain and how they wouldn't let me in the elevator, I stopped. In the meantime, another person had been checked into our room. It was a young girl. Her medical record showed the same diagnosis as mine, only a different, milder stage. But this girl made the strongest impression on me. I tried to sit quietly and relaxed, so as not to betray my bewilderment and the horror I felt at the sight of this poor woman. She could barely make it through the door of the room, she was so unusually large. She was barely up to my elbow in height. It was obvious that she was very, very sick. The girl started talking to the other patients.

It turned out that she had fallen ill with our disease when she was eight years old. They began to treat her almost immediately with hormones and cytostatics. The medication damaged all of her organs and her growth stopped because of the hormones, so she was the same height as an eight-year-old child. Her joints ended up ruined anyway, only now her main disease was joined by concomitant diseases of all the organs she had, and there were multiple side effects from the treatment.

— I take twenty hormone pills a day, I can't take it anymore, nothing helps... I go from one hospital to another... - she turned to me and said: - You're lucky! You should be grateful to your parents that they didn't give you hormonal pills as a child. Otherwise, you would have been like me now, if you had survived, of course... If my parents hadn't treated me, maybe I would have been tall and beautiful, too... - The girl burst into tears. I felt ashamed of myself. I was ashamed that I looked good, and that even though I had got sick when I was only a year old, I still had still grown. I wanted to reassure, to comfort her, but the woman at the window sharply told me, in an orderly tone, - Sit down, let her cry!

I obeyed. I can't put into words how I felt at the time. Those were the thoughts of my parents, who on the one hand had saved my life, but on the other hand I could not understand why my parents, throughout my entire childhood, had made no attempt to treat me, seeing how their child's joints were deteriorating? Seeing a child suffer, seeing a child in pain! Why did they go with the flow? Why let it go? Maybe they knew some secret? Did they know beforehand that the treatment would be worse than the disease itself? Wasn't their heart in tears when they looked at my joints and did nothing to help me? The questions pierced my brain one by one with sharp needles, but I found no answers. Later these questions kept popping up in my mind for about a year, until I stopped them with one sharp phrase: "Stop. Period. Winners are not judged. I am healthy and beautiful. And that's entirely thanks to my parents." But at that moment, in the hospital, I could no longer stay alone with my thoughts. I got out of bed and went to my doctor. I wanted to find out from her what had become of this girl. Would treatment help her now, and maybe she and I had different diagnoses after all, because we are so different! I was shaken to the core that when I entered the doctor's office, stuttering and in some incomprehensible dialect, hardly resembling Russian, I tried to ask her about this girl. The doctor was her attending doctor, too.

— Are you asking about Dasha? - said the doctor.

I nodded quickly.

— What's it to you? Dasha is Dasha. I have half a hospital of patients like Dasha.

— Look at me! Do I look like Dasha? Maybe I have some other diagnosis? - I asked hopefully.

— It's the same, - said the doctor. – Don't think about it! Here's your chart, go for an ultrasound of the veins of the lower limbs. When you get there, give it to the doctor, and then bring it back to me here.

— Look, it really hurts to walk, - I tried to explain my problem to her. – The office you told me to go to is on another floor. I'll have to go there first by the stairs and through a long corridor, and then come back to you again... It really hurts... Maybe I could leave my chart in that office and have a nurse bring it to you later?

— No one here will do anything for you! You've got some nerve! - the doctor shouted in a nasty voice. – All patients here walk by themselves! Do you think you're special?! Get out of here, and quick! We're trying to save your life here, and she has the nerve to talk back!

THE MOON IN THE EIGHTH HOUSE

After taking the chart, I left the doctor's office. Having learned nothing about myself or Dasha, through the intense pain, I slowly hobbled in the right direction. Near the ultrasound room there was a queue. Thankfully there were chairs nearby, and I immediately collapsed on one and looked around: the queue was a few people, taller than Dasha, but also very big, with round faces. They were probably those who had fallen ill as adults. Those waiting were sitting on chairs, reading their charts. I, too, was curious about what the doctor had written in my chart, so I began to read it. On the title page in block letters, it said:

"Ill", then in capital letters - my last name, first name, patronymic. But what was printed next left me absolutely petrified! Namely, the options, one of which the attending physician had to underline in the end. The options were as follows:

1) died after hospitalization;

2) died some time (I don't remember) after hospitalization;

3) exacerbation after the therapy.

In other words, there was simply no "got better after the therapy" or "cured" option for me! I quickly glanced around at all the patients who were waiting for an ultrasound appointment and imagined what kind of answer their doctor would underline for them. I tried to look into the faces of these poor people and see if they were thinking about it, because they, too, were reading their charts, which had the same thing printed on them. But those waiting sat unperturbed and absolutely obedient. I was beginning to get a fever. And it was getting worse. As I left the queue, I jumped up from my chair and, without wasting a minute, headed for my doctor's office. I was very anxious to ask her what fate she had in store for me. What was she going to underline in the end? What kind of therapy had she decided to give me? The same as Dasha's? With these questions I burst into her office.

— Try reading your chart less! It's not written for you, it's written for doctors!- The doctor shouted in her nasty voice.

— If it's not written for me, why the hell are you giving me this card in my hands? - Now I was the one shouting.

— Do you suppose I must carry your chart from office to office myself? All our patients carry their own charts! And no one's complaining! And why didn't you go to the ultrasound?! I told you to!

— That's it, I'm done. I'm going home. I've changed my mind about treatment, - I said knowingly. The doctor pulled her glasses down over her nose:

— What do you mean you've changed your mind? No one will let you out of here. You went to the hospital, that's it, now you'll get treated! The security downstairs won't let you through!

— Do you really think they won't let ME through?! - I threw the chart on the table.

The doctor was clearly nervous and tried to talk me down. Already in a quiet, calm and even conspiratorial voice she said:

— I understand that you must be upset because of Dasha. But forget about her! Nothing can help her anymore. We've been treating her since she was a child.

We put her in the hospital now, because we just have to. She doesn't have a chance. She's already doomed. But you're not! We're going to treat you a little! And then maybe they'll even operate on you. Maybe you'll even walk a little more...

— Treat me?! Same way you treated Dasha?! - I was furious.

— Well, we actually have the same treatment for everyone...

— Can't you fucking see that Dasha and I are different from each other? That I don't need the kind of treatment that Dasha needs?! Who are you trying to make me out to be?! And which option are you going to underline?! - I was screaming my head off. – Where in your fucking chart is the answer that the patient got better?!

The doctor tried to make amends for the conflict:

— Well, hush, hush, you're going to scare the whole hospital. I've never had such violent patients! Actually, no one is picky here, everyone is treated exactly as we say. Everyone understands the severity of their illness, and all the patients pray to us! But you have to understand, silly, that if you leave the hospital now, you'll just die in a couple of months. Your illness is too long... You're doomed. And

I'm giving you a fighting chance...

It was useless to continue the silly dialogue with the dumb doctor. When I opened the door from her office to the corridor, I turned around on the threshold and asked in a calm voice:

— How late are you working today?

— Until six. Why?

— That's okay. I've got a car downstairs. I'll sit there and wait for you to get out of the building. Then I'll run you over to hell and back, and you'll be dead even before I am. Today already."

At these words I left the doctor's office. I didn't even hear if she answered me or not, but she was probably in shock. In any case, she didn't run out into the corridor after me. Even the pain in my hip seemed to have dulled, and my gaze was filled with such anger and hatred for everything that when I approached the elevator, not a single person in a white coat risked telling me that the elevator was for doctors only. Through the security guards and the turntable on the first floor I also got through calmly, confidently and without any problems, no one said a word to me. I got into my car and drove home. My stay in the hospital was about two hours. Two hours of horror, two hours of nightmare – and memories to last a lifetime.

At home, I opened the Internet and began to search for information about my disease and about joint replacement. I firmly decided not to treat my disease, but to replace my hip joint with an artificial one. My man supported me in my decision, and I began my search for a surgeon. The Internet was filled with cheerful, hopeful headlines like "Replace the joint and live without pain" or "We'll give you back the joy of movement" and various articles describing the positive experiences of people who had already been healed. I was encouraged by this information, and in my dreams, I was already walking with a light gait. Now I knew enough about hip arthroplasty that it seemed as if I would be able to assist in such an operation myself. I did not know then that it would be a year and a half before the cherished surgery, before the hour of my "liberation" … that my health would be rapidly deteriorating, inflammatory processes in the body were steadily growing, my leg was shortening, pain was becoming hellish, and the surgeons were refusing me to perform the surgery one after another. I went to all the most famous hospitals in Moscow, but the verdict was the same: "You can't have surgery! You could die!"

I couldn't understand it: Why not? After all, even very old and very sick people have surgeries! And I was young, maybe not particularly healthy… but at that time I was just begging the surgeons to operate on me, saying that I could no longer tolerate this pain, that my physical condition was getting worse catastrophically fast, that if I was not operated on, I could probably really die… After the fifth surgeon refused, I began to think that something was wrong here. It seemed strange to me that I was refused help everywhere. Actually, I have long since become of age, and I was ready to pay a lot of money for the surgery! Trying to find at least some clue, any reason that served as a refusal to operate on me for so many surgeons, it suddenly dawned on me: all the doctors who I went to I always showed them my "medical record", written by the very same doctor. And I could not make out what exactly was written in this record; her handwriting was incredibly sloppy. And I never thought that I would show this scribble to anyone else. After making an appointment with the sixth surgeon on the phone, I went to see him. The surgeon was, to my deepest surprise, extremely nice to me. When he saw my attractive face with make-up, he said good-naturedly:

— Don't worry, we'll fix you, you'll make a runner!

I couldn't believe my ears! I was so happy I was ready to kiss him! But he continued:

— But you have to see my physician first, it's mandatory. Unfortunately, we can't operate on you without him. But don't worry, he's a normal physician, so, everything will be fine. When we operate on you, you'll forget that you had any pain at all!

The physician didn't even ask about my medical record. He just asked about my diagnosis and asked me how old I was when I got sick. After my answer, he said:

— Are you crazy? What operation?! When they cut off your joint, your bones will crumble into flour! You must have osteoporosis in its last stage with such a long period of illness! You can't be operated on, forget it. just live...

I was desperate. Nothing was working. So it wasn't my medical record or at least it wasn't just my medical record. As soon as the doctors found out about my diagnosis and learned the age of the disease, they looked at me like I was nuts, and I would get another rejection. But I had no right to give up, I was in too much pain, so I made an appointment with the seventh surgeon.

My strength was running out, and with indescribably incredible effort, through the agonizing pain, I somehow made it through the long corridor to the surgeon's office. The surgeon was silent, he silently stared at me point-blank, shaking his head, while I, bending over, took small steps to the tiny couch that stood in his office. As I flopped down on it, I groaned in pain and cursed:

— Am I not in a hospital? So, then why the hell do you have such low couches that people with mobility problems can't sit on! I can't get up from it now!

— I'll help you, - the surgeon said kindly. – What happened to you?

— Here, the hip... I need to be operated on...

— I see... What took you so long to decide on the operation? - The surgeon was genuinely surprised. – That's what you've brought yourself to...

At that moment I hated all the doctors in the world. And he was making fun of me as if I've brought myself to this!

— I've brought myself to this?! - I was loudly indignant. – It is the doctors who have brought me to this! No one wants to operate on me! I go to all the doctors and beg for the operation! Please, operate on me, I will sign any papers that I have no claims, any money, please! – Tears were rolling out of my eyes.

The surgeon came over to me and sat down next to me on the couch:

— Don't cry, I'll operate on you... What disease do you have?

That question made my tears dry in an instant, and I said very sharply, even with a smirk:

— I have no idea! What am I, a doctor? How should I know! I've never taken any treatment! You're the doctor, you tell me... What disease do I have?

The surgeon looked at me carefully:

— Well, if you don't want to talk, don't. I'll do the surgery for you. But you'll have to see my physician... it's mandatory. Unfortunately, we can't operate without him.

It was it. The end. I was clearly walking in a vicious circle. It was the limit of all human strength and ability:

— Your physician will tell you that I can't be operated on, - I said indifferently.

— He won't, - the surgeon objected, - he's pretty good... but there's no way to do it without him...

— Okay. Where do I go?

THE MOON IN THE EIGHTH HOUSE

The surgeon wrote down the office number on a piece of paper. I was walking, and my head was completely foggy.

Such hopelessness and despairenveloped me that I hardly felt any pain in my hip.

— Looking for a quick death? - The physician grinned at my question about the surgery. – Do you have any idea what kind of surgery it is? I would have banned them altogether! But surgeons are murderers... No, live your life this way.

When I left the therapist's office, I could have avoided going to the surgeon, but for some reason my legs took me to him.

— Well? What did the physician say? - the surgeon asked me, rotating thoughtfully in his chair and rubbing a ballpoint pen in his hands.

What I answered him at that very moment shocked me, above all:

— Your physician said that I can't have surgery with YOU, that I would die because of YOU during the surgery, because apparently, YOU can't operate...

At the same moment, the ballpoint pen from the surgeon's hand flew with all its force into the wall and, upon impact, was shattered into small pieces:

— Is he out of his fucking mind? Fuck him! Don't listen to him! Do you know how many people

THE MOON IN THE EIGHTH HOUSE

I've operated on? And everybody's happy. I'll operate on you without him! What an asshole!

With a decisive gesture, the surgeon dialed a telephone number:

— Hello, I need to operate a young woman, can I put her in your room? That's great. All right, that's it, Thursday it is.

It hit me like a lightning bolt!

— You're going to hospital on Thursday, - the surgeon told me in a stern tone. – They'll take all the tests you need. I will operate on you. Everything will be fine.

You will make a runner!

ROCK'N'ROLL
May of 2013

Soon I'll have my second hip joint replaced. There was a time when I didn't even think that hip joints exist, let alone endoprosthesis! They had never hurt, but were the first to break completely. As I'm watching my life go by, I remember its most beautiful moments, the moments of my wild youth. My friends and I, for example, used to love to climb up on railway bridges, you know, the arch-shaped ones…I recall climbing to the very top of it and the entire area is on your hand. And underneath there was a river running… My hair was fluttering in the wind, and the whole world belonged to me alone! As long as there were no trains of course, because then the bridge began to shake and holding on to it became very difficult; and the roofs of the train carriages flashed before your eyes so quickly that your head became dizzy, and the best-case scenario is that you could easily slip down into the river. Yeah, not really the best-case. Slipping into the river from that height equals imminent death. Especially for me, since I can't swim. So yeah, we knew how to have fun. My generation is a product of a different age. My youth took place during the crazy 90s, the good years! Back then all the hippies from Moscow and Saint-Petersburg knew me. I was a hipster, wore a black leather jacket, studied at the "Red Alchemist" rock lyceum in guitar and drums class. My youth was everyday parties, concerts, motorbike shows and absolute freedom! My pictures were published in the "Iron March" magazine, and every Thursday at night the TV showed a fifteen-minute-long programme with the same name about our hipster life where, let me be honest, my happy face would pop up constantly. My mum used to watch these programmes and take Corvalol.

Back then I used to date a lot of guys. You know, you're young, there's beer, romance with a guitar and bass drums. But as time went on, I got older. The decorations around me, my interests and my social circle changed. Now I don't have the slightest idea where my friends, admirers and fans from that time are… And only with one person from that careless fun life we've carried our memories and stayed in contact through these years. It is Dima. Dima is a musician. He was in love with me, and wrote songs about me which his band then performed at their concerts. Dima was in love with me for a very long time. He was in love with me when I dated other guys and he kept on loving me when I got married. He loved me when, after a few years of marriage, I left my husband for another man, and he continued to love me all those years while I was living with that man. And even when I left that man too, he still loved me… Almost all of the men I was with knew Dima, he didn't try to hide the fact that he was in love with me from them. I was his muse. Some time ago Dima got married and (hopefully) became a decent family man. He is still the same. Just like in my youth. He still performs with his band and he still invites me to "hit some rock'n'roll". And I will, of course; just like the good years, I'll hit the drums! Afterwards. I've got to fix my leg first.

I remember how it was last time: after the rehabilitation period, my soul was yearning to play some drums, although I had been doing pretty fine without them for the past few years. But not just to play, but, as we said it in my youth, "to go wild" or "have a blast". Except my appearance wasn't really fitting for that "blast" anymore. Well, think about it: a tight skirt, high heels, such a kitty-cat girl… And not that I played all that well after a year out of practice. But I was unstoppable. I started taking drum lessons from two different famous musicians, and so it began. Oh, how we played! What a wonderful time it was! I could write a book about it! But I won't. I want to keep this era of my beautiful life in secret, so that only I could reminisce it some time in a cold winter, in a soft armchair, cozily covered in a warm blanket with a glass of red wine to the sounds of unforgettable jazz…

A wall of memories from my old years stands before my eyes. I can't even fall asleep, still remembering… I know what it is… I'm simply terrified. I have a serious surgery soon. No, it's not the pain I'm scared of… of course not. It's just that I can feel that it will… It will once again be a cruel war. Once again, I'll have literally survive and fight for my life. It will very difficult. Maybe, even more difficult than the last time… Yes, I am scared, but I am ready. I can't hide or run away from it. And I'll be sure to fight through this with dignity. At least, I'll try… Yeah… my optimism has run out. But it will pass. It's only, as my friends and I put it, a "stars' joke".

Today I was driving around the night city of Moscow and saw an old Volga, GAZ-21. What a great car it is! I have one, very precious memory related to a car like that. I have this story written somewhere, I'll have to rummage through my old diaries and reinforce it in my memory. Such pleasant memories as this are a cure for my wounded soul.…

My personal diary
May of 2013

THE MOON IN THE EIGHTH HOUSE

GAZ-21. THE OLD "VOLGA"

I was walking home from my friend's house on a beautiful spring day; back then I was in my early twenties. Outside my doorway I saw an old, ugly, first generation "Zhiguli" car with a "FOR SALE" sign on it. My neighbor Gena, the owner of that beauty, was bustling around the car. After greeting me, he kicked a wheel of his "kopeck"-model car and complained to me that no one was willing to buy that beauty, when really, he needed the money. Then he turned to his car and, waving his fist, promised that in case of "non-sale" he would take the poor car to the woods and burn it. I felt so sorry for this tiny little baby vehicle that out of nowhere I said, "Do you want me to sell this car for you?"

And that's where it all started. I began selling secondhand cars. Gena's car sold for triple the price. And Gena, all happy and joyful, immediately brought me a crowd of his car-owning friends, who also needed to sell their cars as soon as possible. Step-by-step, I began to develop a database of clients and used cars. And in the north of Moscow, Lyosha was also working just like me, having entered this business by accident; our paths crossed and we became partners. Lyosha was my best business associate! We made a perfect team and together we would sell any car for any price! Lyosha and I didn't need words to understand each other, even our gesticulation was the same! (Without any rehearsing!) Customers, especially when couples arrived, after one look at us wouldn't leave without buying. And mind you, Lyosha and I had a strictly business relationship. And if, as happened much more often, our clients happened to be men, who normally came in a group of three, typically unfriendly buyers (the first one being the car body expert, the second one being the engine expert, and the third one being the one who wanted to actually buy the car), I was the leading act in our pair with Lyosha. And these three big men, upon seeing me, a young, attractive harmless girl, grew kinder right in front of my eyes. They straightened up, pulled their bellies in, squared their shoulders, and tried peacocking, acting like some English gentlemen. Generally, all the sales took place near Lyosha's house, and Lyosha's neighbors, as well as many other acquaintances, even before the "action" began, before the buyers arrived, asked in droves for permission to stand aside and watch how a tiny girl, that was me, would sell the next masterpiece of domestic automobile industry. So, we always had an audience, which made the show even more interesting! All my selling techniques were different. When I spoke with the clients, inspiration just came to me. And normally, the car body experts, who would come to me, never examined the body of the car, much less knelt down or in assumed any other awkward poses in front of me just to check the underside of the car for rot and holes. The engine experts wouldn't even open the hood and would buy cars from me without looking, often paying me even more on purpose, showing that for "real men" money wasn't a problem!

The sales were in full swing. We had accumulated a decent database of old cars; we were selling an average of one car a day, and we were receiving a large number of sale requests on a daily basis. So, we had work for many months ahead. And then, one beautiful day in December, some old woman called me and asked me to sell her and her husband's GAZ-21. An old Volga. The car was a rarity, with the gearbox located on the steering wheel, leather sofas inside, a deer figurine on the hood, the car still had the old black license plates. Perfect! There was also a problem: the car had not been driven for thirty years, although it looked good, not a single scratch and still with its original paint (almost intact!). I put the old woman's car on my list and promised to "keep it in mind". At the time I didn't have a client interested in a GAZ-21, but there were plenty of other cars, so, I was selling them. But the old lady took her time to call me every day and complain about her difficult, cash-strapped situation, so I decided to meet her after all, take a look at the car and help the old lady in need. Around that time, I was married with Edik. With his eyes closed, Edik could assemble and disassemble any car. He wasn't a part of my business plan, but when I needed to start some ancient, broken car that no one had ever managed to fix, I would ask Edik to help me. And he would start it without its key and without the right parts in the shortest time possible. So, I took Edik with me, and we went to Kupavna, a suburb of Moscow, to examine the Volga. The old couple welcomed us warmly. The old man vividly recalled the old days, when he proudly drove his car, while his wife told me her life story since birth several times. For that reason, Edik and I never got to see the car, our only wish at that moment was to say goodbye to them as soon as possible. These old guys wanted $300 for their Volga. The car was parked in a garage of a private old wooden house. The garage door hadn't been opened in about thirty years and was densely overgrown with shrubs and various weeds. We entered the garage from inside the house, honestly speaking, I didn't pay any attention to this important detail at the time. All we saw during our visit was that the car looked just fine for its age. The only document the lady showed me was a technical passport from the early seventies of the 20th century. I called Lyosha and told him about the car. And then the most interesting part happened. Just a few days later I got a call from Lyosha:

— Lena, hi! The buyers are on their way! They're already around Moscow! - Lyosha shouted in panic.

— Lyosha! What buyers? What do you mean, they're already on their way? Where did they come from?

— There's no time to explain! They'll be in Moscow soon! Tell me the address, where in Kupavna... I'm on my way. Yes, just don't be mad, I told them that the car is in very good condition and has been removed from the register... I didn't know that they would just take off and come from Kamchatka to Moscow! They just called me and said they would be in Moscow in about three hours... so don't be mad, we could probably get it started somehow?

— Are you out of your mind?! - I was furious. – And removing it from the register?! What were you

THE MOON IN THE EIGHTH HOUSE

ing the car. Lyosha, you take the grandma! Sit, drink tea with her, listen to all her stories about life. But don't let her get in the way here. Well, you, Igor, are lucky! Today you are not just the audience, you're taking part in the whole process! I like you, so welcome to the team! You're dealing with the old man. He's changed his mind about selling the car, and I don't care how or what you tell him! But make sure he doesn't leave the room, hold him hostage, just don't overdo it! He is still old, after all... I'm going to a traffic police station to bring the cops to deregister the car here. When I get here with the cops, I want you all to sit quietly in the house, without the old man or his wife in sight. That's it, I'm off to the traffic police!

— What if the traffic cops refuse to go? – Igor hesitated.

— Don't be silly, - Lyosha interjected sharply. - Would you say no to a girl like that?

After Lyosha's words, it was a matter of honor for me to bring the traffic police here by all means!

— Yes or no, we'll talk about it later, when we've successfully sold the car! - I said in a confident voice. – And now that the roles have been distributed, let's get started!

After my fiery speech, the eyes of all the members of our gang glittered, and Igor was happy! Probably it had been a long time since something interesting happened to him, so his soul was hungry for adventures, and he took up the task he had been assigned with great enthusiasm. Rubbing his hands with pleasure, he headed for the house with the words, "Hey, Grandpa," he said, stretching his words conspiratorially, "I'm coming to see you... where are you hiding?"

I went to the traffic police. The car was registered thirty kilometers away from Kupavna. All the way to my destination, I was trying to think of a cover story. What to tell the traffic cops, why I need to remove the car from the register at home, and even without the presence of the owner. Well, if the first question could still be somehow resolved - the car was not running, not that it could drive on its own ... then how do I explain to the cops why I'm the one taking the car off the register, even though I have nothing to do with it? And what happened to the owner? Or maybe I did something to him? And will the cops even go with me thirty kilometers away? In this weather? My thoughts didn't align into a believable story. Having come up with nothing, I decisively opened the door to the traffic police chief's office. I entered with a proud look and without any idea of what I was about to tell him, I said hello. And then there it was! My cue! Opposite from the chief's desk, there were two huge tanks with fish.

— Oh my God! Cool fish you have here! What a beauty! - I made my voice as enthusiastic as possible. The chief smiled, quickly jumped up from his desk and walked over to the tanks:

— Do you like it? They're my soft spot! I have two more tanks at home. But you can't put these and these fish in the same tank, because these can eat those over there. And that fish is a rare specimen, almost no one has them, but I do!

The chief was clearly living in his own world. He talked and talked excitedly about his fish: How and what he fed them, which fish got along and which didn't, and occasionally I would exclaim enthusiastically: "No way! Really? Crazy! You're absolutely right! Beautiful!"

Time was running out. The buyers were probably quite close to Moscow already, and nothing had been done yet. But then the chief, totally content, said:

— Well, enough talking about the fish! You had some business here, didn't you?

So, I said the first thing that came into my head:

— My... grandfather is dying... - I was shocked at myself.

- Oh, I'm so sorry... How can I help you? - The chief got sincerely sad.

Fish are a great thing, after all!

— My grandma is all alone, – I took a deep breath – She doesn't have much money, so she asked me to help her sell Grandpa's car, so she could at least get some. And the car is old, with black license plates, it doesn't run, and Grandpa is in a bad condition, he can't get it off the register... but I've already found a buyer. The car's in our garage, in Kupavna; grandpa is there too, but he's barely sane anymore...

The chief with a decisive gesture pressed the phone button: Vodopyanov, come here, - and looking at me fondly, he added: Don't worry, I understand, we'll get everything done.

THE MOON IN THE EIGHTH HOUSE

A young traffic cop, criminal expert Valery Vodopyanov, entered the office.

— You're going with this girl, - he pointed at me - You are to do whatever she tells you to do.

Victory! Hooray! After saying goodbye to the chief and waving goodbye to his fish, Vodopyanov and I drove to Kupavna. On the way, trying to stick to the cover story, I told him that he needed to remove the car from the register, and that he had no reason to worry, there were absolutely no problems with the car's documents, grandpa had bought it from a Soviet general, the most honest man of all. Vodopyanov seemed relaxed and at peace and was not yet worried. When I arrived at the place, I saw that the garage gate was open, the weeds and bushes had been pulled out, and the snow had been cleared away. Edik was lying under the car, fixing something. When he saw me with a cop, Edik froze in fear, but at the same moment he quickly realized that everything was going according to the plan, so he relaxed and continued to fix the car. We crossed eyes with Edik, and I realized that everything was fine: Lyosha was listening to old lady's stories, and Igor… well, I didn't know exactly what he was doing there with the old man, but it was fine as long as he was under control. "What a good team I have!", - I thought, - "They did everything right! Well done!"

I spoke casually to Vodopyanov, handed him the car documents, smiled my most charming smile, and said:

— Here are all the documents, it's all good, just like I said.

At this phrase of mine, Lyosha and Grandma came into the garage, and she decided to put her cents into the conversation:

— Oh, I completely forgot to tell you! Don't look at the documents. The marking doesn't match anyway. My idiot of a husband stole the engine from someone else and put it in. So, now the engine has a different number, so don't look at the papers!

The atmosphere in the garage dropped dead silent. Edik went under the car and held his breath; Lyosha's jaw dropped as he was standing absolutely still; Vodopyanov looked me straight in the eyes, absolutely dumbfounded, a question in his eyes clearly evident. Everyone was waiting for my reaction.

— Lyosha, take Grandma away, - I said as I felt my legs buckle again.

— Great job, Grandma, well done! Don't you know when it's time to steady your tongue? - Lyosha ushered the old woman.

And since the traffic cop was still standing there, bewildered and completely confused, I said:

— Valery, it's no big deal, the numbers don't match, but who cares? It's nothing. It happens... Remember what your boss told you? Do whatever I tell you to do. So do your job. The chief knows...

Vodopyanov, though incredulous, but probably remembering his boss's words, slowly began to check the license plates. It seemed as if everything was getting better, and even Edik gathered enough courage and stuck his half-torso out from under the car again. The cop was silently putting some notes in the documents, not paying attention to the mismatch of the numbers. I sighed in relief. "That was close," I thought.

But then suddenly, from somewhere above, probably the attic, we heard heart-rending screams: "You won't do shit without me! You won't get away with this easy! I'll have you all locked up! I own the car! You can't sell it without me! No chance!"

The cop jumped away from the car, Edik slid back underneath the car body on the skids and hid.

What was that? – Vodopyanov pointed his finger at the ceiling, with terror in his eyes – Did you hear that? Who's screaming? What is going on in the attic? What the hell is going on here?

The operation was in jeopardy! I realized that the cop suspected that the most horrible crime of the whole century was taking place here in the garage, and that he was a direct participant. I think I was blotching with fear, I had to make a decision immediately, before Vodopyanov came to his senses, called for reinforcements and before we all got busted here. Meanwhile the anxious cop started rushing around the garage, casting frightened glances at the ceiling and listening to the shouts coming from the attic. This time it was Igor who shouted: "Too late, old man! Shut up already. We have a traffic cop in the garage, and he will deregister your car for good without you! We got it covered! You have no idea who we are! You don't want to mess with us!" I was close to fainting, but with an incredible effort of will, I gathered all my patience and composure together, and with a pleasant smile on my face I said to Vodopyanov:

— Don't worry so much, - I walked up to him on trembling legs and took his hand -Don't mind him. They told you... Grandpa's dying... he's in agony... have you taken the car off the register yet?

— I have...

— Good. You're the best.

— Now you have to get a license from the traffic police, - Muttered the policeman.

— Then what are we waiting for? Let's go... Go get in the car and sit there quietly, I'll be right there.

Vodopyanov, obeying my command silently,

without asking questions, left to get into my car. Meanwhile I needed to blow off some steam. I pounced furiously on Edik, who got out from under the car saying, "Wow, I almost shit myself... My whole life ran before my eyes...".

Edik removed some part from under the hood and started twisting it in his hands. I wasn't letting up.

— What kind of idiots are you?! You're all dumbasses! You've been given simple tasks! And what do we have? One of you let the old hag into the garage and the other one can't get an old man to stay still. And you, what's wrong? What's taking so long? When are you going to start the damn car? The buyers are almost here! And what's that in your hand?

— The starter, I took it off. They don't make them like that anymore. Look how old it... Before he could finish his sentence, the old iron starter broke in half in Edik's hands, like a bar of chocolate, before our astonished eyes. –"Oops..." – the only thing Edik had time to say. But sensing his near and painful death at my hands, Edik immediately began to vividly explain himself:

— It wasn't me! It really wasn't me; it did it itself... because it's ancient... Just imagine how old it was! No way you can buy a thing like that nowadays...

Once again, my legs went limp. I didn't have time to kill Edik, I had to go to the traffic police. And it was dangerous to leave Vodopyanov alone in my car

Without supervision. What if he radioed back to some other cop that the crime of the century was taking place right here, in a garage near Moscow?

— Okay listen! I don't even want to think about it. I'm going to take Vodopyanov, get the plate, and when I come back here, I want the Volga to be on the street and on the road. That's final!

I ran out of the garage, jumped into my car, gestured the pale cop to chill out, and we took off to the traffic police. Vodopyanov tried not to talk to me on the way, sitting all bleak, probably thinking all the way, what he was so deeply involved in, and how he was going to get out of it all.

The light of the gasoline indicator flashed:

— Got to fill up the tank, we're running out of gas, - I said, and with a sharp turn of the steering wheel, I turned to a gas station. At that very moment, with absolute terror, I discovered that my purse with the money and the documents wasn't in the car. I had left it in the garage! Oh no! A few sharp and loud curses came out of my mouth. Vodopyanov jumped up. Oh, how funny all of it would be, if it weren't so sad! I looked at the poor cop, who, at this point, had been expecting literally anything from me. Now, car owners will probably understand! How many times I've been fleeced by the traffic police! And most times it was cheaper to pay than to mess with them. Now the situation was quite the opposite.

— You got any cash? - I asked the terrified policeman.

— How much? – Vodopyanov pulled out his wallet. It seemed that at that moment he was ready to give me all the money he had, just to never see me again.

- Ten liters of AI-92... Go fill it up, huh?

Vodopyanov nodded and went to fill up the tank. But then I realized that I would have to pay a tax for the license plate. Vodopyanov came back.

— The tax is on you, too.

— Okay, okay. I got it. I'll pay...

— Thanks.

— Don't you have any more relatives in agony whose stolen cars I'll have to deregister? - The policeman asked me tactfully.

— No, don't worry. I promise.

The cop exhaled. Vodopyanov, a Saint that he was, paid me all the receipts, and I got in line. There were a whole lot of people in the traffic police, and only one window was operating for issuing documents. But my kind traffic cop came to my rescue here again.

Probably, in order to get over with me faster so that his eyes would never see me again, he had a word at that window, so that they would quickly give me my license plates, and then, he came up to me with a sly smile and said:

— Now, when they announce the last name of the one from the attic, you go and get your license plate.

And then a man's voice boomed out of the document-issuing window across the hall:

— Fedkin!

I shouted back:

— It's me! I'm Fedkin! I'm here!

The car owners waiting in line, looking at me distrustfully, parted and let me through to the window. We had a short constructive dialogue with the man at the window. For several seconds he stared at me in silence, evidently trying to recognize me as an elderly man. Then, apparently, he did, and with a completely impassive face, he loudly stated:

— You are Fedkin.
— Yes!
— Ivan Nikitich?
— Yes!
— Born in 1926?
— Yes!

— Here, Mr Fedkin, sign here, here is your license plate.

When I got the plate from the traffic police and raced back to Kupavna, I saw (no way!) that the car was back on the road and functioning. Lyosha had tied it to his minibus and pulled it out of the garage. I was happy! The car looked amazing, it worked, and I don't know what black magic Edik started it with, but the fact remained. No sooner had I had time to express my admiration to Edik for repairing the car than the buyers arrived. Had they arrived five minutes earlier, they would have seen not the most pleasant image, namely, how a minibus was trying to get their new car out of the garage. But everything happened as it should have.

The buyers turned out to be the nicest people who were ready to jump into their newly purchased vehicle and drive it to their faraway home. We signed the car purchase agreement last minute as well, before closing, and in general everything went very well. The customers paid us off and left satisfied.

We went inside the house. I needed to catch my breath. Igor had taken the old man out of the attic. I don't know exactly what Igor had done to Grandpa, but he was unrecognizable! It was like he'd been replaced. He became a completely calm and kindhearted man. Really, no point in yelling now, right? It's no use! The show's over. The old man got his $300 and was happy. He shook hands with all of us and thanked us profusely. A few days later, the buyers called. The car was 59 kilometers away from their house in Kamchatka. There was some ticking in the engine. But they were happy all the same, and so were we.

I happen to be in Kupavna from time to time. There's a fish factory there, and the town sells really good fish, the tastiest fish I've ever eaten. Several times I drove past the house where the Kupavna events unfolded. Immediately, images of that epic day came to mind. A day I will never forget. And probably everyone involved

in those events, just like me, still remembers that fun story. And perhaps, Vodopyanov, too.

THE GOD OF KNEES

The day of my hospitalization was approaching.

A law banning smoking in all public places had been released in Russia. Hospitals were almost the first to be ban smoking. The nursing staff were deprived of their smoking rooms, and the unlucky smokers were forced not only to run out into the street to smoke, but also to go far beyond the gates of the hospital itself, since its territory was also subject to prohibition.

I smoked, too. An avid smoker. For a long time, I had been trying to get rid of this disgusting habit, but somehow it didn't work out. I started it back in the nineties, when our whole country was endlessly smoking. And when society viewed a normal non-smoker as a sick person who had to quit smoking due to health reasons. Soon after the "Non-smoking Law" was passed, I finally gave up smoking for good. No turning back. But that happened later, but for now...

— Well, well, well - I lit a cigarette, thinking out loud to my husband - Can you imagine, what if there is a most difficult surgery happening, like mine, for example? The operating room is full of surgeons and anesthesiologists... and the operation is so long, it takes hours... - I paused for a puff and continued:

Probably before, in such a situation, smoking doctors could reach the smoking room and run back to the operating room... And now what? What to do? After all, while the smoking medics are outside the hospital and even for a quick smoke... anything could happen to the patient... How awful... And probably the doctors will have to restrain from smoking, and wait in anticipation... and that's a scary thing. Because then they will be trying to finish the surgery as soon as possible, and whatever happens ... just to finish it all as soon as possible and finally smoke! And it wasn't even a matter of unprofessionalism, but simply of nicotine addiction! - My own words made me feel uncomfortable. I was imagining it all too vividly.

— Yes, it's not very pleasant, - my husband agreed, - I know that after I smoke, after about twenty minutes, I take another one, and that occupies your mind, until you take a drag...

My husband was supposed to be in the hospital with me almost at all times, sometimes even staying there with me overnight. Obviously, the issue of smoking was very relevant for him and me, so I decided to talk to Mr. M. about it.

— We can't smoke in the hospital, - the surgeon told me firmly - and if your husband stays here overnight, he can't leave the hospital either, he has to wait. That's the law now, I don't like it myself either...

The whole hospital was abundantly covered with posters and signs prohibiting smoking. The crossed-out cigarette in a red circle was hanging everywhere: on all the doors to the offices, on the walls in the corridors, in the toilets.

— Although you know... - Mr. M. smiled squinting slyly - Maybe I could help you!

— Oh, thank you so much, that would be great!

— You're welcome! - I got excited.

— The whole gynecology department adores me! They all love with me! I'll send you there, they'll let you smoke inside if I ask them to! They won't say no to me. I'm their hero. But when they send you off to the traumatology department, don't say anything, pretend you don't know you're going to be in gynecology. Okay? I'll get the word across to the girls there. Don't worry. Well, of course, for a reasonable price...

— I understand, I understand! Of course! Tell me how much to pay, and I will! As long as there would be no problems, and I'd be able to open a window in the room to smoke...

— Okay, - the surgeon continued firmly, - You don't have to pay anybody anything. You give me the money, and I'll take care of it.

— If you say so... I just want everything to be perfect...

— It's all settled then! One thing though, now you'll have to pay this - Mr. M. wrote on a piece of paper a sum almost twice as big as the amount that was originally estimated for the hip replacement surgery and an ordinary bed in an ordinary, non-smoking room in the traumatology department,

— But officially you will pay the amount we agreed on at the beginning, you understand, don't you?

— Well, of course, I understand. It's a deal... - I was willing to pay that money for the peace of my mind and my comfort, - Thank you very much!

— You're welcome, - Mr. M. was being flirty, and then said in a solemn voice, - It's just that the girls in gynecology won't give me a break! They love me a lot! I'm the best man they could have!

The day of hospitalization came. Right away I want to mention that I looked very good, and a person who did not know and did not understand my problem would never have noticed that I had a slight limp. I presented myself gracefully. The thing is, I already knew at the first joint pain what it was and that "it wasn't going to just pass on its own." I took an x-ray. The x-ray confirmed my diagnosis. An operation was necessary. That same afternoon I contacted my surgeon and asked him to have the surgery as soon as possible, to "have another go", so to say. Pictures of my past life rose before my eyes one after another, as I anticipated another operation of the century, and, of course, I anticipated crazy mad doctors, surgery refusals, wishing me a quick and painful death ... I anticipated many things...

But the most terrible memory of the last operation was the intubation. Because I had to do it myself! It wasn't believable at all. The last time the anesthesiologists didn't manage their job, explaining that probably my trachea was deformed and they couldn't get it. Then they told me that "only I can get the tube inside because only I know my swallowing mechanism..." I agree, kind of crazy. And perhaps, my dear readers, it seems unbelievable to you, but believe me, that's exactly what happened. And when I, trembling with fear and the unreal horror that lay ahead of me, asked my attending physician, at the time of my first surgery:

— Is there such a thing as patients anesthetizing themselves?

— First of all, they don't anesthetize, they intubate! - the doctor corrected me, - There is a big difference!

And secondly, no, of course not! Although in theory, in our student-books it is possible. But in practice, no one has ever done it, so, you are the first! You could say you're a pioneer! You're lucky!

Well, yes! Lucky was an understatement! And if all normal people, before any, even the simplest surgery, had a nurse who would come and give them an injection, so that the anxious patients would relax, stop being afraid and drift off to a half-asleep state; well, I had to be wide awake last time, because I had to sit with a perfectly straight back and get the tube into my own trachea. At least the fear of my surgery of the highest level of difficulty was completely replaced by a new, even wilder fear. The fear of my own intubation. I remember how, sitting on the operating table, with my eyes bulging with terror, with my trembling hands on this tube, I tried to persuade the doctors not to conduct such experiments on me, not to do it. After all, there are other types of anesthesia that do not involve a trachea! But the doctors were relentless. For some reason, they did not even try to consider other types of anesthesia for me. My teeth were chattering with fear and my tongue was slurring, but I still made one more attempt to explain to the doctors that I might not be able to handle this task, because I am not a doctor!

— You want me to damage my lungs? I skipped anatomy in school! I don't even know where my lungs are! In fact, how would you even know if I hit my lungs with this tube? - My whole body was trembling with horror, because I really didn't understand the methodology of this procedure, and I really couldn't say with absolute certainty where my lungs were.

— It's simple, - some doctor told me from the operating room. – If your eyes roll back, you're in trouble!

— If my eyes roll? Are you being serious? – I was close to fainting.

— Of course, I'm serious - answered the same nonchalant doctor. – When your eyes roll up, you'll stop breathing, and we'll do the breathing instead of you. Less talking, chop-chop! - the doctor hurried me.

— I can't do it! I just can't! - I could feel that the words tumble and rumble inside my mouth. My teeth were chattering and my hands were shaking. Basically, the doctors were asking me to take my own life, and I had never been suicidal, so the prospect of putting a tube in my own lungs and suffocating to death was unbearable for me.

— I can't do it! - stuttering, I tried to repeat myself. – I can't!

— Hurry up! Get that tube inside! The sooner you start, the sooner you leave - the doctor seemed to be trying to joke.

I sat on the operating table, clutching the damn tube with my trembling hands, and tapping my teeth. I couldn't make up my mind, but suddenly a loud voice from some doctor brought me out of my uncontrollable state of fear:

— All right! If you don't get it inside, we're all leaving! You can't have the surgery any other way. There's no other way. You either do it yourself or you don't. Is that clear? Make up your mind. You have five seconds!

And not a second later, I opened my mouth and put the tube in. I don't remember what happened next. I woke up in the intensive care unit.

I told Mr. M. this terrible story and asked his permission to talk to the anesthesiologist before the surgery. I was not ready to intubate myself again,

I really wanted the anesthesiologist to give me their word that this would not happen to me this time. But Mr. M. shrugged it off. He switched to the first-name basis with me.

— Nothing's gonna happen to you, there's no need for you to talk to our anesthesiologist.

— Please, - I insisted, – It's very important to me!

— No, come on, stop it! Don't think about it at all; anesthesia is not your problem at all!

— But that was my problem last time! I need to tell that to the anesthesiologist, - I urged Mr. M., but he clearly had other things on his mind,

— That's it, I don't have time to talk to you, I have work to do. We have the best anesthesiologist; everything will be fine.

I called Mr. G., the surgeon who operated on me last time and who decided to put me in this hospital. I expressed my concerns about the anesthesia to him as well, but Mr. G. reassured me saying:

— Nothing like that will ever happen to you again, don't worry. The hospital where you'll be staying in has the best equipment in Moscow. The latest equipment.

In theory, I could operate on you under any conditions. But the most important thing for me is that your past-surgery days go well. This hospital is the best there is. So don't worry, I'm sure they have a very good anesthesiologist. Deal?

— Deal... - I said quietly.

— So, you go to the hospital on Thursday, and I operate on you on Friday. All according to plan.

After collecting the right amount of money, my husband and I arrived at the hospital early Thursday morning. I looked very well. The pain in my hip was severe, but still, I wanted to go to the hospital beautiful; it gave me some courage and self-confidence,

confidence that I would survive and get through all of it. We took the things we needed for the hospital including crutches, since after the operation, I was supposed to start learning to walk, right in the hospital. The cab driver who came to pick us up was very surprised when he found out that I was the one who needed the crutches, because he didn't have the slightest idea that I was a person who was going to have a difficult surgery. My mind was restless and in fear, and I was in no mood at all. This is understandable. The surgery I was to undergo was not an easy one, with a difficult and painful rehabilitation period. Therefore, I was not at all happy about it. In the emergency room I was assigned to the traumatology department. After paying the agreed amount of money at the cashier's desk, my husband and I went up to the gynecology floor, which we had previously agreed with Mr. M. I was going to check in first and then, to avoid walking around the hospital with my things, go to the surgeon and bring him the money, for which he promised me smoking opportunities in the room.

A nurse met me on the floor of the gynecology department and escorted me to my room.

— Thank you, - I said, - so in this room we can open the window and have a quiet smoke, right?

— Are you out of your mind? - the nurse raised her voice rudely, - Are you crazy?

— I am sane, - I interrupted the nurse, - Why are you yelling at me?

— Well, I don't think you're sane if you say things like that! - the nurse wouldn't let up,

— Okay, don't raise your voice at me! - I tried to smooth things over, because the nurse might not have been aware of our arrangement with Mr. M., - The surgeon gave me permission.

— Oh, so the surgeon said it was okay?! Well, would you look at that! - the nurse was yelling, smugly and very loudly, - The surgeon gave her permission! - and turning around, clearly making a show, she turned to the patients standing in the corridor of the department, — Did you hear that? The surgeon gave her permission!

The nurse's facial expressions were disgusting. She stretched a sarcastic, ugly grin and, turning to me again, said,

— Don't even think they'll let you smoke in here! - the nurse got overly familiar with me, - Just you wait until I get the head doctor of the department! We'll see what she has to say!

The nurse walked briskly and briskly somewhere. My husband and I stood there in utter bewilderment.

The hope was that the head of the department would come. and our conflict with the nurse would be resolved.

The head doctor, a middle-aged blonde with sharp and petite features, did not come alone, but was accompanied by several female medics. All of their faces were excited, aggressive, and even somewhat combative.

— There she is! Look at her! - With a finger pointed at me, the nurse turned to the head doctor, - It's her!

— Hello - I nodded and said hello.

— Okay, so - She looked at me sarcastically from head to toe, and the doctor retorted, - You can't smoke here! And I do not care who promised you what! Who does he think he is to be giving any permission in my department? You can stay in his department and do whatever the hell you two want! But no! He's not gonna set himself up like that! Why would he want all that trouble?! That old dog!

— People nowadays are completely shameless! - Another female medic picked up on it, - We let you stay in this department, and that's what you do?! Ask for more?! "Can I smoke here?", my ass! She's got some nerve!

All the doctors nodded vividly, agreeing loudly and very angrily. The women in white coats were yelling and screaming, getting random female patients

of the gynecology department in conversation from time to time and describing to them in a nutshell my incredible rudeness and my obscene desires.

— And God forbid we catch you smoking! Even one subtle smell of smoke from you or your husband, - she hissed, pointing her head toward my man, - and you're out on the street! And I couldn't care less if you're here for a surgery! You're not on holidays here! We'll throw you onto a stretcher and kick you the hell out of here! You understand?

— And no one's gonna baby you here! – shouted a new, squeaking, disgusting voice from the crowd,

- Your surgery's on Friday, and then it's our days-off! So, you're on your own here! And forget about your husband's visits, we will not even let him in at all! And you're on your own in the ICU, too! And if Mr. M. wants you so much, you can stay with him anyway! You're not welcome here!

— Stop! - I shouted sharply, trying to drown out the crowd of insane, angry women, - Everybody, shut up! That's it, I'm leaving! I'm not staying in your hospital!

— That's right! You're not welcome here! Get out of here! - The furious mob of doctors rejoiced in their victory.

My heart was pounding and ready to jump out of my chest, and my head hurt like crazy. The hysterical women were shouting and shrieking. Trying to get through the crowd of angry women in white coats who were deliberately obstructing me, I shouted to my husband - I'm going to the surgeon!

The doctors let me through and switched to my husband. He was saying something to them... But I didn't hear it. My only thought was to run to Mr. M. and tell him what had happened.

— Calm down! Sit down! - Mr. M. said in a harsh and loud voice, - It's nothing serious!

— Nothing serious? - I was outraged, - You should

have heard what they were saying! How they insulted me! How they shouted!

— Don't make things up! - the surgeon snapped at me angrily, - There's no way they would shout or badmouth! Our hospital has a great reputation! I've known these women for years! They are beautiful women!

— I'm not making anything up! They're yelling at my husband right now!

— That's it, I don't want to hear anything! Go back to your room! You have a surgery tomorrow! I don't have time to talk to you here, I'm actually working! - Mr. M. shouted at me and turned to his computer's screen, where the page of a social media site was open.

— They also said I can't smoke... - I tried to continue the conversation.

— Oh, yeah, the smoking thing didn't work out... I forgot to tell you... That's okay! That's all right, even better for your health. I said quiet! Our conversation is over. At least you have a room in there, did you see how great it is? I got it especially for you. So, the money we agreed on, consider it payment for the room. Not everyone can get it! - Mr. M. said without taking his eyes off the webpage on his computer.

— You know what, I'm sorry, but I've changed my mind about the surgery - I said confidently.

— What do you mean you've changed your mind? Everything's ready, you've paid the money! Go back to your room and don't be stupid! All right, I'll talk to the girls and tell them to be nice to you since you're not too happy. Although I'm sure you're making it up. These women are saints!

— Did I stutter? I will not have the surgery here! After today I just can't do it. That's it, I'm calling my surgeon.

After this phrase of mine, Mr. M. finally broke away from social media and, changing his venomously aggressive tone to a kind and understanding one, said very nicely:

— Wait, no need to call your surgeon. Don't bother him. What if he's in major surgery right now? We can figure this out on our own. Wait for me here in my office, I'll go to the gynecology department and take care of everything. And when I get there, we'll decide whether or not to call your surgeon. Okay?

— Please, you have to understand. I've made up my mind - I tried to get through to Mr. M., - Even if the whole gynecology department altogether suddenly apologizes to me, I won't stay here. If they apologize, their ego will be hurt, and then they will definitely follow through with all the threats they've said! And I need good past-surgery care. Please, let me just go home, that's it.

— Wait! Just Stay in the office! Come on, please! Well, I'm begging you! The best surgeon in Russia is begging you! Begging! Take a seat. Don't make any hasty decisions! I'll be right there; I won't be long. Just don't call anyone! Do you hear me?! Please! - At these words Mr. M. ran out of his office. After a few minutes, the surgeon returned and said triumphantly,

— That's it! I've taken care of everything. I talked to the girls. You just had a misunderstanding! They're very kind and very nice! And you snapped at them, offended them... But no offense taken, so you don't have to worry! We're all human... everyone understands! You're just nervous. It's understandable, you have a surgery tomorrow. Anyway, go to your room. And yes, by the way, - Mr. M. said turning back to his computer to look at the website, - I could have kept it away from you, but I will tell you, because I see that you're all wound up... Your surgeon just called while I was in gynecology. Anyway, I described him the situation in a nutshell, and he said you shouldn't make quick decisions. Tomorrow is the operation. Just as planned. He can't change his schedule because of your whims and fancies. That's it. Now go to your room - he added dismissively, - Come on! Hurry, hurry! Can't you see I'm working!

For a few seconds I was still sitting in my chair in the doctor's office, without any idea what to do. I saw and felt the surgeon's insincerity. Literally instantly, out of the blue, I suddenly understood and even envisioned Mr. M. running out of the office, calling my surgeon, and vividly telling him probably in foul language the story of my disgusting behavior... I looked at Mr. M. He was nervous, biting his lips, poking at some pictures on the social networking site. Mr. M. was performing a cruel show for me. He probably thought I would believe the whole farce. He even made me feel guilt! And what was really striking is not that he lied to my surgeon on the phone about me, but that he was trying to convince me that I had offended the poor women in the gynecology department! Well, if I was guilty, then there was no need to be ceremonious with me, so Mr. M. decided to let himself talk to me in such a harsh and rude tone, so that I fully felt all my insignificance, to apologize and shut up. So, the question is, What for? Well, a patient changes their mind about their surgery... well, why not just let them go! Why all this drama? My dear readers, there was only one possible answer: Mr. M. had already planned how he was going to spend the money from my surgery, and it was a lot of money, so he could not lose it. And sad as it sounds, that's exactly what happened.

— And what did you tell my surgeon, may I ask? Did you tell him that I wouldn't be operated here? - I turned calmly to Mr. M.

— That's none of your business! I'm not your subordinate to report to you! - The surgeon said exasperatedly, clicking robotically his mouse on the images on the social media page, - Go to your room, do not interfere with my work!

— Here's what's gonna happen. I'm not going to have surgery here. You're being unacceptably rude to me. I'm going to call my surgeon myself and explain the situation to him - At these words I got up from my chair and was about to leave the office when Mr. M. very quickly and energetically blocked my way,

— Sit down, please! - He said quite kindly, - Let's talk!

— What do you mean talk? - It would be funny if it weren't so sad, - Weren't you just trying to kick me out? Am I not standing in the way of your work? - I said nodding toward the open social networking page.

— Am I really being rude? You're just imagining things! Well, why are you so uptight? You're nervous. Sit here with me, calm down a little...

The overly emotional surgeon with very active facial expressions and intermittent body movements took me by the hands and put me back in the chair. He began to walk restlessly and quickly himself from side to side in the office. It was clear that Mr. M. was under a great deal of stress. He was asking me questions and answering them himself,

— Are you scared? Well, don't be. And the girls in gynecology are very nice. You shouldn't have. So, are you still nervous? Have you calmed down a bit? I can see you're calm!

Mr. M. kept talking and talking, and his monologue was long. Several times I tried to say something along the lines of "I'm not nervous," but it was all in vain. He simply wouldn't listen to me and continued his speech,

— I'm the best surgeon ever! I'm the God of knees! I am the God, - and, probably to make his words sound more convincing, he raised his hands up and, looking at the ceiling, as like into the sky, once again he said very loudly, solemnly and with expression, - I am the God of knees! God of knees!

— I'm very happy for you! - I yelled louder than the smug surgeon, - This is very cool! It really is! But I'm actually here for the hip joint! I don't really care about my knees right now!

After these words, the surgeon went silent and froze for a couple of seconds. Then, quickly coming to his senses, and Mr. M. did everything very quickly, briskly, in a showing off manner, he waved his hand and said,

That's right, your hip joint replacement! Well, that's a piece of cake then! For I am the God of knees - he said as he raised his hands up again and looked up at the ceiling, - and your hip is nothing to me! It's a minor operation for me! So, you should be happy that I'm going to be there operating on you along with your surgeon!

— Wouldn't my surgeon be operating alone? - I felt uncomfortable with the idea that such an impulsive and unfriendly God of knees would only get in the way in the operating room.

— Why do you think he sent you to me? Because I'm the best surgeon! And he doesn't want to take any risks, he's afraid! You have a very serious illness, and you've been sick for a long time. And people like you are just my thing! I operate tons of patients like you. No one wants to take responsibility for people like you.

The surgeon went off on a tangent and, without any hesitation, using the worst profanities that I'm not going to include here, he rudely bashed people with serious health issues who needed joint replacements:

— So, you're lucky! Since I'll be operating along with your surgeon, you'll still be able to walk on your feet! - he said proudly.

— That's all great, of course, but as you can see, I'm on my own feet right now in front of you now, even though my surgeon operated alone last time.

— It's been years since then! - Mr. M. interrupted me loudly and sharply, - it's been what, eight years? Do you really think your disease is slowing its pace? It's progressing! Progressing rapidly! Him, operating on you, was bullshit! It was total bullshit! Now it's a really big surgery. That's why he asked for my help. He can't handle it on his own.

— So, you think I'm a very sick person? - I asked the surgeon, - Then why do all the numerous tests that I took in order to go to your hospital, as well as the

Medical reports of all the doctors say otherwise?

Indeed, my tests and medical reports were perfect.

— It doesn't mean anything! It's all nonsense! You're very sick! Very sick! And don't listen to anyone who says you're not! Then they're lying! And your surgeon just can't deal with you alone, he doesn't have much experience - Mr. M. concluded.

— Well, I really don't know what to tell you, - I exhaled, – I'm sorry. I'm sorry about everything. I'm sorry to bother you, but I'm really not ready for the surgery.

— This again? - Mr. M. started rushing around his office again, - I've just explained it to you - the surgeon put his hands out in front of him and started moving his fingers - your surgeon can't operate without me! What do you not understand?

— I understand... I'm going, okay? - I got up slowly from my chair and said, - Excuse me again, goodbye...

— Go to your room! You have an operation tomorrow! - The surgeon shouted behind my back.

— You'll never guess what happened here! - When my husband saw me, he started talking excitedly about what the women in white coats had told him, - It was a nightmare! They attacked me... you can't stay here!

— All right, talk about it later. Did Mr. M. come here? Talked to them? - I asked my husband, - I didn't see him. These hags were yelling and insulting you and me! I'm actually shocked...

— That's it, let's get out of here, I will not have surgery here; go get your things, let's get out of this hellhole quickly - I said in a confident tone, - Now somehow, we need to turn in these papers, which I was given, and most importantly we need to return our money.

My husband took the bags with our things and the crutches. Suddenly the door of the room opened, and a young, smiling girl in a white coat walked in.

— Hello! - she said, smiling sweetly.

— Hello, who are you? - I asked without smiling at all.

— I'm your anesthesiologist, - the girl answered, smiling pleasantly again, - Mr. M. just sent me to you, saying that you were very scared of the operation and that I should talk to you.

To say that I was shocked is not to say anything. When I really asked him for an appointment with the anesthesiologist, he bluntly and rudely refused me.

And now, when I told him a hundred times that I would not stay in this hospital – Voilà!

— Thank you for coming in, but I'm not going to have the surgery here, I've changed my mind, I'm going home. By the way, do you know where I should turn in this card?

— You've changed your mind? Oh, I see - the girl said, still smiling, - it's just that Mr. M. probably doesn't know yet. And you should take the card to the emergency room and tell them that you've changed your mind. They will do whatever they need to do with it there... And then go to Mr. M. for his signature. He has to sign it, or you won't get your money back.

— Thank you very much for the information - I said, smiling at the pretty girl, - I'm sorry to bother you.

— No big deal, goodbye!

We said goodbye to that pleasant girl and, alone in the room together with my husband, we began to discuss an escape plan.

— So, - I said, attentively assessing the situation, - Mr. M. won't let me go nicely, it's already obvious. I wouldn't even be surprised if a nurse came here now to prepare me for the operation... See what a fuss we've made! He even sent an anesthesiologist right away!

The door of the room opened, and another young girl in a white robe walked in. She said hello.

— Hi... - I nodded, - Who are you?

— I'm a nurse, Mr. M. sent me to you! He told me to give you an enema... You have an operation tomorrow...

My husband wanted to say something, but I squeezed his hand.

— Oh? So early? As far as I'm concerned, this procedure has to be done late at night, before going to bed, and after dinner? It's only 1:00 in the afternoon! I was actually going to eat! And I'll be eating more during the day, too! Let's not do it now, shall we?

— All right, let's do it tonight, - the nurse agreed.

I was surprised too, as Mr. M. said, "No talking! Just do it!".

The nurse left the room.

— I'm so impressed... - my husband was so shocked by the current situation that he had no other words.

— I'm going to call my surgeon and tell him everything. And you rush to the emergency room, tell them that we've changed our mind about the operation.

But how are we going to get Mr. M.'s signature... I have no idea...

My husband grabbed the chart and rushed to the emergency room. I called my surgeon and told him everything. My surgeon listened to me calmly,

— Well, it's your decision. I'll operate on you at another hospital. It's just that the equipment here is the best, and that another hospital is soviet run-down type.

— I don't care! - I shouted into the phone, - Anywhere, but here! Please!

— Well, all right, I'll call Mr. M. myself and tell him you're going home. Don't worry about it.

I was in pure bliss!

— Will you please apologize to Mr. M. for bothering him?

— Okay.

I must say that I did not have to explain to my surgeon all the details of what was going on in that horrible hospital during this conversation, and I told my surgeon about Mr. M. later, not then. After that phone conversation, I calmed down. That's fine. There is another hospital where Mr. G. will operate on me. Everything is fine. My husband will come now, we'll go with him to Mr. M.'s office for his signature, take our money back and go home.

Abruptly opening the door, Mr. M. ran into the room:

— What was that you said to your surgeon? - Mr. M. shouted and gesticulated widely, - We had agreed that you were going to have surgery tomorrow!

— We didn't agree on anything! I've told you a hundred times that I've changed my mind about the surgery!

Mr. M. rushed around the room:

— "Don't you understand what I told you? I am the God of knees! I'm the best surgeon!"

— And I'm very happy for you, but I'm going home!

— You're not going anywhere! That's it! You're not getting out of here! You're my feeding hand! - and after mumbling to himself, he stormed out of the room. My heart raced. How could I get a signature from him? He's completely mental. I was getting scared of him. And that line about me being "his feeding hand" was, of course, too much. I sat and thought about my next plan of action. Suddenly the door to the room swung open, and Mr. M. walked in again:

— We just talked to your surgeon again, and he's coming to operate on you tomorrow. That's final. It's settled.

— Look, Mr. M., what did you tell him this time?! I told you I'm going home! Let me go! - I was outraged beyond measure.

— Both your surgeon and I are convinced that you are hysterical! He's coming to operate on you tomorrow.

— Me? Hysterical? You're the one who's hysterical! - My tears were forming out of desperation.

— Maybe I should tell the nurse to give you a shot? - Mr. M. was not giving up.

— I'm going to call my surgeon now. That's it, I can't take it anymore and I'm going to tell him everything! - I said and picked up the phone.

— Go ahead, call him! He'll simply refuse to operate on a lunatic like you at all! And soon you won't be able to walk at all! You'll be bedridden forever! And no one will help you! At all! I promise you that much! Make the call. He's already regretted getting involved with you a thousand times. We talked, he was completely shocked by your misconduct! - smiling maliciously, aggressively and very rudely Mr. M. smirked.

— I'm not staying here anyway! My husband went to the emergency room with the card...

— Oh, so that's how it is! - Mr. M. interrupted me sharply, - So, you really decided to go that far! Well! It's your own fault! - Mr. M.'s eyes started to glaze over, - No one will be returning you your money without my signature! And my workday just finished! That's it! I'm not in the hospital! I'm somewhere away! I won't be here tomorrow or the day after that. In fact, I'll never be here for you. You'll be coming here for months trying to catch me. Do you understand?! What goes around, comes around... Go on and try and get your money back! I'll show you!

Mr. M. ran out of the room, cursing and waving his hands. I called my surgeon again. I was shaking. Now I told him everything.

— Lena, this is a hospital, not a prison, - Mr. G. Told me after listening to me, - He'll sign everything. They'll give you your money back, don't worry!

My husband returned.

— It's done. Now all you need is Mr. M.'s signature, and that's it, home sweet home!

On the way to the surgeon's office, I told my husband everything that had happened in his absence.

— What a hellhole. I had no idea it could be like this!

Mr. M.'s office was locked. I dialed his number on the phone.

— I told you loud and clear! - the surgeon yelled into the receiver, - I left! You'll have to catch me! That's it, bye!

I cursed loudly at the entire hospital. It was very difficult for me to stand outside the closed office and it was also very difficult for me to walk, because I was scheduled for a joint replacement surgery. My leg was in great pain. The thought of "trying to catch my money" was just unbearable. Not only was every step

very painful, but the hospital was three hours away from my home due to traffic jams. I collapsed in my chair:

— I need a smoke! - I said loudly.

— Quiet - my husband put his index finger to his lips, - Somebody's going to hear you! Let's go outside and smoke there...

— No... too far away for me! I won't make it! - The pain in my hip joint was severe.

— Well, let's sit and rest for a while ... and then we'll go outside.

— No, I want to smoke now! - I said confidently,

- Come on! I know where we can smoke!

We went up to the floor of the gynecology department. There were no people in white coats in the corridor. Quickly we snuck into the bathroom. We were both very uncomfortable with the fact that we were breaking the law, but this was revenge! It was sweet revenge!

— Now let's try to get our money without Mr. M.'s signature - I said, and we headed for the cash register.

When I approached the cash register and made sure that the girl at the window was looking right at me, I pretended to be on the phone with Mr. M. At the same time, without stopping the imaginary conversation, I gave my card to the cashier at the window, pointed to my phone and said,

— Miss, Mr. M. is away now. He'll be here in fifteen minutes to sign everything. I've got him on the phone right now! He said I could get my money.

The girl nodded vividly and gave me all my money without hesitation. Only when my husband and I walked out of the hospital gates did we finally realize that we were free. It was a wonderful feeling! I spent half a day in the "lair" of the God of knees, but the memories were going to stay for a lifetime.

THE MOON IN THE EIGHTH HOUSE

The astrological transit aspect of the operation has already formed in the sky. So, it will be soon. Very soon. Mr. G. found me another hospital. I will be calling Mr. B., the head of traumatology at that hospital, one of these days. So, I needed that time for something. But for what? I looked at my astrological forecast. Amidst the difficult aspects of the struggle, there was an aspect of some great joy... but from where? What joy is there for me right now?

Weirdly, the joy is coming from the "house of disease" ... Something meaningful and wonderful is about to happen in that "house" that will make me very happy, even though I am preparing for a surgery of the highest level of difficult! Now that was new! I'm going to find out what it is one of these days. I even cheered up! I'm looking forward to the gift of the universe! At such a difficult and hard time for me, it's especially appreciated.

My personal diary.
June 2013

CRIMINAL DEN

In the meantime... I just remembered another interesting story that happened long ago, when our country had already lived through the wild nineties and had just entered the threshold of the new millennium, in the noughties. At that time, the amazing vivacity of my character, pure enthusiasm and complete inability to sit still constantly threw me to expand my activities. I had selling stalls at the market, where as an individual entrepreneur I sold household chemicals and toilet paper, and a store, which I modestly named after myself and which soon safely went bankrupt, and, of course, the sale of unforgettable used cars. The cars were sold with ease and playfulness. In fact, you could tell absolutely any story of my sales, and it would be a lot of fun. Every time I drove out to sell a car, I said I was going for the "deal of the century." And it wasn't because I was getting some big money, no, of course not! The money was okay – it just that it was not the main thing. The main thing was the emotions and adrenaline that I experienced each time, because everything was always "on the line". After all, absolutely all deals were under the threat of failure! The car would not start, then something would fall off during the inspection... then at the last moment it would turn out that the carwas without documents or had no owner. Often, I wouldn't see the car before it was sold. Probably it was the adrenaline that my young soul was asking for at the time, and I was happy to give it in full. When I sold fewer than a dozen of old cars, I already had a reputation of a girl "who can sell any dead car to anyone for any money". Such an honorable reputation and the corresponding attitude to me not only flattered my self-esteem very much, but also suggested that I would have to "keep up the mark", not to relax and at all costs continue to be the best in my business, so as not to disappoint the enthusiastic crowd and the legend created around my persona. And that's how it was: sales were "on the brink" but great, buyers often told me only after the paperwork was done, "Well, now show me what I bought?"

All in all, everything was fun, until one call came:

— Hello, hello! Are you the guy who sells cars? - A pleasant male voice asked me.

— Yes! What kind of car do you want?

— I need a model "six" Zhiguli, not older than two years. And in perfect condition! A good body and running gear! I want to hop in and go. And only green. Do you have one?"

I wondered. I didn't have any green ones.

— Would dark-purple be okay?

— No! I want green! I was told you could find me a car, you were recommended to me. Find me a car! I want a functional car, and I want it green! I got $2,300. I need a really nice car!

Yes, he had enough money to buy a nice, running car, but there was a problem with the color. I didn't have any green cars.

— I'll use my own channels to find you a car, and you call me back tomorrow. I hope I'll have something for you.

That was the end of the deal. I called my partner Lesha. He called all the car markets we knew and found about five two-year-old green models "six" in excellent condition. In my mind, I had already ticked off a potentially sold car. Never before have I offered a client so many cars to choose from! Usually, they took what they were given. And here they had a range!

The buyer, whose pleasant voice I had heard on the phone, came with his friend to meet me. Both young men's names were Pasha. Two Pashas. And as it turned out later, that wasn't their only resemblance. I do not know what "interest groups" they met in, but they both had been in the war: one in Afghanistan and the other in Yugoslavia, and both had been badly shell-shocked. And so, these two enlightened Pashas, obviously waiting for some kind of trick or deception, came to meet me to choose a green car. After getting them in my car and picking up Lyosha on the way, we drove to our first destination, where the coveted car was waiting for us. It was a sunny winter day. The car was cleaned and polished, it seemed to be well-prepared for sale. It started with a half-turn, and its color was really green. I smiled: "What a nice day!"

While both Pashas, standing a meter away from the "six", were piercing it with a silent stare, Lyosha came up to me and said joyfully, but quietly, almost in a whisper:

— The car is so cool! At least it's not that bad! Still, it's nice to sell good cars

— Yes, - I agreed, - our customers today are very lucky. It's a beautiful car! I wish it were always like this!

— Look at it, it's not even overpainted!

— Yes, I see, I see, it's not even scratched anywhere! I've never seen a Zhiguli in such a beautiful condition! The car is a beauty!

Lyosha was clearly pleased with himself, because he was the one who had found this car, and all four others, too.

— I don't think there's any point in going to see the other cars. I don't think those cars will be any better han this one - Lyosha told me.

— I agree, - I confirmed, – Then let's get the paperwork done and go home!

My mood was great! The beautiful winter sunny morning promised an easy and pleasant "deal of the century. I closed my eyes and put my face in the sunshine. The car was gorgeous, I wouldn't even have to tell the buyers anything, they could see it for themselves, of course they would buy it now...

— The car is garbage!

It was like an electric shock. At the very second, I opened my eyes and saw both of them standing in the same place, the same meter away from the car, talking loudly:

— Total garbage! - said the first Pasha.

— That's terrible! What do you think this is, a car? I don't need that kind of junk! It's worth 500 bucks at most - Pasha agreed.

— You didn't even go near the car... what are you talking about? - I was indignant.

— What's the point of going near it?! We can see from here that it's total trash!

— Well, if this car is garbage, - said Lesha, - then all the others won't suit you at all. It's a very good car.

What's wrong with it?

— Wrong! - shouted one of the Pashas, – I want to buy a good car, and you're giving me some bullshit. Are you trying to trick us? I warn you; we are not to be trifled with! We were in the war! We're shell-shocked!

The second Pasha also joined in the conversation in a high-pitched tone. Both of them were clearly hungry for some kind of big showdown, the kind of brawls that were so common in the nineties. But nothing of the kind was in my and Lyosha's plans, so we tried to placate the furious buyers and promised to show them the other cars. At other viewings, the Pashas behaved horribly. They were loudly shouting obscenities and got into a fight with the employees of the car market on ethnic grounds. Eventually they were separated, but the Pashas were insanely rowdy, one of them occasionally displaying his big knife in a threatening manner. Lyosha and I realized that the Pashas simply missed the war and that we would not be able to sell them our car without casualties. And the sale wasn't our priority! We wanted to stay alive! There was no point in taking such insane buyers to another viewing. It was clear that the next car would only make them angrier, and God forbid, someone would get hurt. But the Pashas were not going to let us go, they apparently decided that now we simply had to find them a car that would satisfy them. Thankfully the day was coming to an end, and having explained to the shell-shocked buyers that we would not have time this evening to look at the remaining cars and it was better to postpone everything to tomorrow, Pashas agreed, but with the proviso that we would not be able to hide from them and that they, the great soldiers and just "the right guys", would find us, and then we would pay. We went home. From the next day on, Pashas kept calling me on my cell phone. They didn't have Lyosha's phone, so they took all their anger and aggression out on me. Most of the time I didn't answer the phone, but sometimes I did, saying something that occurred to me at the time, stalling for time. I really hoped that they would give up on me and buy a car somewhere else. But no such luck! The Pashas were clearly having so much fun! They were interested in pretending to be tough and menacing guys and scaring me, a young, fragile girl.

I was driving in my car on the Gorky Highway and turned up the music to ignore Pasha's incessant calls: "How can I make them stop? - There must be some way to get rid of these crazy people," I thought.

No sooner had I thought about it than I saw a green car on the side of the highway, along the wooden old houses, and a stand next to it with a big sign saying "For Sale"! I sharply slammed the brakes. As I got out of the car and approached the green fence, I was thrilled to find that it was a model "six" Zhiguli. It looked great on the outside, but as I walked around it in a circle, I noticed that the windows had different numbers ofr the year of manufacture. So, the windows had been removed from other cars. The paint job was fresh and perfect. "The car clearly had a complicated history of its own; what had happened to it, and how many cars it had been assembled from, remained a mystery. I walked resolutely to the fence of the house and was about to press the bell, when someone honked at me from behind. When I turned around, I saw an older man behind the wheel of a blue model "nine", who gestured for me get in the car. I did.

— Are you here to see me? - smiling sweetly and clearly flirting with me, the man asked. His hands and fingers were covered with thieves' tattoos.

— I guess, if that's what you're selling, - I said, pointing to the six, - I want to buy it.

— I'm selling! - the man got excited, - A wonderful car! Not beaten, not painted! Garage storage! Used a little, a woman drove it!

I smiled. They were trying to fool me. It was so funny! Personally, I had never used such stupid and deceptive sales techniques, but I had heard them very often from other salesmen. What's more, everyone said exactly what the man told me. Word for word! In general, with the phrase "a woman drove it" they would sell any car, even the most beat-up one. And if the car looked good externally, the seller would say in a convincing and firm voice: "A woman drove it! And women drive rarely and carefully, they don't race!" If the car showed any dents, the salesman explained with a guilty half-smile: "Well, what do you want, a woman drove it! You know how they drive: here and there they scratch the car...". In both cases, the cars were beaten and broken, and the dishonest seller was trying to hide the unpleasant truth under the disguise of "a woman's driving".

— How much do you want for your car? - I asked.

— 500 dollars - the man replied - But I can drop it if you find faults!

— Why are the windows from different cars? Did a "woman drive it"? - I smiled and sneered. The man hesitated and fidgeted in his seat, my question clearly stumping him.

— Okay, don't make it up. It all makes sense to me. You want $2,300 for the car? - I meant what I said.

— How? It's unrealistic... I want to, of course... But it's such trash... Who needs it...Who are you?

The man became visibly nervous, and I laughed.

— Calm down, I'm not here for you, I'm here for the car. Tomorrow you'll get $2,300 for your car. But I'm going to need your help.

The man's eyes sparkled, he got excited, squared his shoulders, and said in anticipation of the greatest con:

— I'm ready! What do I have to do? I'll do anything! Just sell this junk! $2,300? Are there really such idiots? What do you want for it?

— I don't want any money, - I said confidently, - think of it as a goodwill gesture. The clients are two creepy guys, and I need them to leave me alone. You'll be able to talk to them in "your way", "in your own way" in case of anything, won't you? You know how to do that, don't you?

— Yes, we can do that! - Rubbing his hands with delight, probably remembering the old days, the man was happy.

— That's the deal. What's the paperwork on it? What year is it really?

— Eighty-six...

— Oh, just great...

— What... it won't work? - The man got upset.

— It'll work out, it's even more interesting.

At that very moment, Pasha called for the hundredth time. I didn't have a plan yet, but I picked up the phone and looked my new acquaintance in the eye and told the annoying Pasha:

— Well, I've found you a car! My uncle is selling it!

My new acquaintance stretched out in a smile and, without taking his eyes off me, listening, held his breath.

— I'd forgotten all about him! And the fact that he has a green model "six"! It's a great car, you'll love it! The man's giving it to you for 2,300. He wanted more, but I talked him into it. I'll see you tomorrow at the place.

The man sat there in mute delight.

— What is your name? - I asked.

— Alexander

— Uncle Sasha, then. Uncle's a relative, after all... And I'm Lena. Well, Uncle Sasha, find me some young, strong guy. You got any?

Uncle Sasha immediately called someone:

— Vasya, come here quickly, I'm at the gate in the car. Come on!

A minute later a young man came out of the gate, looking like a huge werewolf, so scary and terrifying was his appearance. Vasya was about two meters tall, broad-shouldered, with a very dysfunctional face, and also with tattoos on his fingers. Only Vasya had far fewer tattoos than Uncle Sasha, from which I deduced that Vasya was still an inexperienced novice criminal, while Uncle Sasha was probably respected in his circles and tough.

— I wonder how many more there are behind the fence? Where did I end up, anyway? - I thought. But it was too late to retreat. Looking at the Vasya-werewolf, the plan emerged. We got out of the car.

— Will he do? - Uncle Sasha asked me, nodding his head toward the monster.

— Quite!

— Then command, my dear! He's all yours!

Huge Vasya stood in silence and waited for instructions.

— So, Vasya, tomorrow the buyers for the model "six" are coming, and I need you to not let them get ahold of the car documents under any circumstances. You'll just stand there, keep the documents in your hands and keep quiet! Understand?

— I see, - Vasya's voice matched his appearance perfectly.

— Silence! Don't talk to anyone! - I repeated, as I doubted that the man-mountain understood what he was talking about.

— I see, - Vasya said again without any emotion.

— Then we'll act according to the situation. In the meantime, all you have on you are the documents!

— I see.

After sending Vasya back behind the fence, Uncle Sasha and I began discussing the details of the "deal of the century". It turned out that he had his own notary, who would write out a general power of attorney for the car without waiting in line or "unnecessary attention". In those days, people often bought cars by general power of attorney, it was easier that way. Hardly anyone was ready to go through the terrible and painful procedure of registration at the SAI. Therefore, this "six" had the license plate, and this fact did not raise any questions at all.

I looked behind the fence and was stunned! I thought it was an ordinary house standing there: a vegetable garden, seedbeds... There was no such thing! There were various broken car bodies, spare parts and tires scattered all over the place. Both garages were open. In one of them, two people of Caucasian nationality were painting some sort of car, and in the other, a damaged car was being dented. The work was in full swing. And I was shocked.

— Is it possible to put everything away by tomorrow? I mean, like, inside the garages or something? Don't scare the customers, they're already sick in the head... and if everyone sees this... They have to think that you're my perfectly normal uncle, without any

THE MOON IN THE EIGHTH HOUSE

criminal business. The "Six" is your personal car... Although...

My gaze fell on Uncle Sasha's tattooed hands.

— It's not a problem! I have a huge area behind my house, and there are a few more cars parked there. We'll put something there, hide something in the garages. We'll do it. Don't worry, honey.

— At least like that. We can't take clients on the side of the road.

Outside the gate, Uncle Sasha and I walked up to the car:

— Don't forget, Uncle Sasha, to take the car out of the gate. Or let's bring it in now, why is it standing there? Where are the keys?

Uncle Sasha staggered in one place, and I was struck with a terrible suspicion:

— Don't tell me... Isn't it on the move?

— Don't worry, Alik will start it up tomorrow. He's the only one who knows how to turn her on.

— Who is this Alik?

— Alik. He's Armenian. He's in the garage. You want me to get him?

— Don't. But can it at least drive?

— Hell, if I know... Maybe it'll go thirty kilometers...

— Okay, I don't want to think about it. Anyway, now they'll come for you, if anything... How can it be possible?! You have so many people working for you, and you sell cars so unprofessionally and stupidly? - I was very surprised, - "Garage storage", "driven by a woman"... Do people still fall for that?

— Yes, cars are not selling well, what can I say - complained Uncle Sasha. – People have become clever, you can't just screw them over now!

It became quite obvious to me that I was in the den of some incomprehensible local crooks near Moscow. And my job was to get the two insane, concussed men who posed a threat to me together with the nicest people in tattoos to leave gracefully. And since the Pashas didn't want to buy really nice cars, let them buy this one, of incomprehensible origin, and finally leave me alone.

The day of the "deal of the century" came. I arrived before the buyers. I made sure the area was cleaned up and the car was parked in front of the house. Uncle Sasha had even shaved for the occasion. I told all the workers to sit quietly in the garage and not to show their faces in the territory. Only Uncle Sasha and I, Vasya the werewolf, and Alik stayed, because he was the only one who knew how to start the "six". Alik was no longer a young man and his age could be just a friend of my uncle, who happened to visit him. Vasya rolled up the car documents and stood silently at the side. Everyone was waiting and worried. I was more worried than the others, because it was my game, my "deal of the century," for which I had promised Uncle Sasha $2,300.

Both Pashas arrived. I was "in shape" and totally confident. Since the Pashas were calling really good cars "junk," I wondered what they would say about this one. My calculation was correct:

— Oh, what a nice car! It's not beat up! Not painted! Super! - Pasha walked around the car in circles, stroking its body with affectionate enthusiasm.

— You see - one Pasha turned to me, - I told you that you would find me a car anyway! When I demand something from people, they always do it!

I stood there smiling sweetly. Uncle Sasha came up to me:

— Why don't you tell them anything about the car? - He whispered softly in my ear, - Maybe I should tell them about "garage storage" or that my "wife drove it"?"

— Are you out of your mind? Don't you dare, - I hissed. – Don't say anything at all. You're going to blow the whole deal for me!

I was in the middle of a conversation with the two of them.

— It looks like a garage-kept car - the first Pasha praised the "six".

— Yes! And your wife probably drove it? - Pasha asked, turning to Uncle Sasha.

Uncle Sasha, totally bewildered and confused, nodded vividly:

— You're really something, honey! - he whispered enthusiastically to me. It wasn't me; it was them, - I answered smiling.

They opened the hood, and Alik got behind the wheel and started the car. To be honest, it didn't run very well, but he kept praising the six, and I kept quiet and didn't mind.

— What about the documentation? - One of the Pashas asked.

— Of course, it's clean, - I answered in a knowing tone, - Well, let's go to the notary, if you like it? My uncle might change his mind about selling his car so cheaply!

— Let's go! Let's go! Great car! - The Pashas were all over the place talking about the "six".

But suddenly one of the Pashas turned his attention to the wheels:

— Oh, why is the rubber so bad? It's icy outside, and the rubber is completely bald!

Just when I opened my mouth to say something clever about it, the Armenian, Alik, who was forbidden to say anything, interrupted:

— I'm going to get you something! Wait! - he said in broken Russian and ran off.

I got worried, "What else is he up to? He's going to ruin the whole deal for me with his behavior!"

Alik came running in a minute. He had a new studded wheel in his hands:

— Do you like wheels like that? - he asked.

I looked at the wheel and thought, "I wish I could have those wheels! Mine were almost worn down to the cord. And I would have sold those wheels to Pashas anyway!"

— Oh! Nice wheels! They're great! - Pasha shouted.

Even too great, - I thought enviously.

— I can put them on for you right now. Would you like it? - Alik asked kindly.

— Of course, we do! Put it on! - the Pashas rejoiced. Uncle Sasha's notary was five minutes from home, so in order not to lose time I suggested:

— Well, if you like everything, before my uncle changes his mind, let's go and go to the notary and do the paperwork quickly. And when we get there, the car will already be on good wheels. Get in my car! - I opened the door of my car with a decisive gesture.

The joyful Pashas got into the car, one in the front seat, the other in the back. I nodded my head and called out to Vasya. Vasya somehow crammed himself in the back of my car, next to the other Pasha, and we drove off. All the way to the notary, Pasha happily chirped about the "six" and how people always do for them whatever they ask, clearly alluding to me. Vasya sat in silence, staring at one point in front of him.

— I want to see the documents! - Pasha suddenly exclaimed.

— Vasya has them, - I said without taking my eyes off the road.

Vasya continued to sit silently and didn't even blink an eye.

— Vasya, let me see the documents, - Pasha said to Vasya.

In response, Pasha again received complete silence, and Vasya didn't even change his posture, continuing to sit and stare at one point. I was laughing! I held on with the last bit of my strength not to burst into laughter. Well done, Vasya! Well done! I could not even think that my task of "silence and do not say anything" would be taken so literally!

— What, not saying anything? - I asked Pasha, barely able to contain my laughter and trying to make a serious face.

— Silence. Va-a-a-a-sya. Vasya! He's silent! - Pasha threw up his hands. – And why is he silent?

— It's a long story... He doesn't talk at all! Ever since he was a kid... - just don't laugh!

But he has the documents! Tell him to let me see it!

— He also can't hear you, Pasha! He knows he's going to the notary, and he has to give the documents to the notary, my uncle told him so. It's his son. Vasya listens to his father and he's scared. Don't worry, you'll see your documents! And if something is wrong in the documents, no notary will execute any deal for you.

You understand that, don't you? Although if you want, you can try, of course, to take the documents away from Vasya...

I was on a roll! Pasha looked at Vasya. Vasya was twice his size. After hesitating for a few seconds, Pasha waved his hand:

— All right, let him guard our documents, they'll be safer that way!

When I arrived at the notary and ran into a long line, I sat both of the Pashas down in their chairs and said:

— Now Vasya and I are going to try to get through without waiting in line, I don't want to keep you waiting.

— That's right, - the Pashas got cocky. – We don't like to wait. Go and think of something, let them make it quicker for us! We still have a lot to do!

Completely disgusting clients were making themselves out to be very important people. But it's okay, the notary had an agreement, of course, Vasya and I went in without waiting in line, and we were quickly granted a general power of attorney. In the notary's office Vasya and I laughed, merrily remembering the whole spectacle that was going on in my car. Vasya turned out to be quite a normal person, and I even began to like him.

Vasya, you need to repeat the feat once again! Sit and be silent! - I laughed my ass off and said:

— You're really good at it!

— I got it, no problem! I even liked it! - Vasya's eyes were shining, he obviously liked the task.

All the way back, Vasya continued to sit, silently staring at one point. Pasha didn't risk asking him for his papers. We arrived at Uncle Sasha's house, Alik met us and told us that he had changed the wheels and warmed up the car. The Pashas settled up with Uncle Sasha, and I took the documents from Vasya and gave them to the new owners of the "six":

— Well, that's it, goodbye! - I said goodbye to Pashas.

— I told you you'd find me a car anyway - the buyers decided to show off one last time.

— Good luck on the roads! - I smiled and waved. The model "six" car started up and drove off. Uncle Sasha and Alik came up to me.

— Alik - Uncle Sasha said to him as he looked at the departing car. – Can it make it to the Moscow Circle Road on those wheels?

— No, not to the Moscow Ring Road, too far away... - answered Alik, looking after the moving away "six".

— What are you talking about? - I didn't understand. – Didn't you get new wheels?!

— Eh! What new ones?! - Alik was indignant, - I have only one new good wheel, I show it to all the customers!

— Wait, - I was confused, - I saw it when we arrived, the car was on spikes!

— Oh, I'm the one who riveted the bald tires with a gun! I got spikes; I got a gun! Why not rivet if the customer wants studded ones!

— In ten minutes, all their spikes will fall off, - Uncle Sasha explained to me.

— No, in twenty, - said Alik.

— Well, you're clowns, gentlemen! - I laughed. – And if they noticed that you had tricked them and riveted their bald wheels? How would you get out of it?

— No one ever notices, - objected Uncle Sasha. – You didn't notice, either...

That's right, I hadn't noticed. I had never even heard of it. The workers came out of the garages. All of them, happy and excited, were saying something, pointing in my direction. A phone rang. It was Pasha calling:

— Hello! The car is an '86!, - he shouted into the receiver.

— Don't yell like that... really? - I asked nonchalantly.

— Yes, yes! Eighty-six! And I wanted a two-year-old!

— Well, not everything happens the way we want it to. What can we do...But it's green... If you have any complaints, come back here, they will explain everything to you in your own language.

— We have no complaints...

After I got off the phone, I looked around: about fifteen workers were standing about twenty meters away, whispering admiringly, pointing their fingers in my direction. "Silent" Vasya, laughing loudly and gesticulating widely, was telling two guys about our trip in bad language, and they were smiling and throwing respectful glances at me. Uncle Sasha was shining like a polished piece of metal:

— Let my eagles at least wash your car! - he suggested.

— Don't, the rust would be too noticeable, and the paint would peel off. I'll go - I decided to say goodbye to Uncle Sasha quickly.

— Wait, why don't we paint your car? Or do you want us to build you a new one?

— No thanks, I like mine! I'll go!

— Wait, don't go! Aren't you interested in a "Moskvich-2141"? Don't you have any customers? I couldn't sell it for a month! And there's a "Svyatogor"... Why don't you take a look at it? How can we do without you? You rubbed it in your faces... I want to tell you something... Wait, don't go... The car you sold, Vasya stole it a couple of months ago...

— Okay! Uncle Sasha, don't tell me anything, I don't want to know, don't involve me in your business! - I sharply interrupted the criminal's story.

— Just listen, don't interrupt, that's not the point... That's not what I mean... We reconstructed the whole thing, of course. But it turned out that Vasya had screwed up. Death is too kind for him, he yanked the wrong car! He hurt some serious people. Do you know how much trouble I've been in because of that car? The cops came to me every day, wondering if it was this car or that... When cops come to you all the time, you know... I paid them so much money... and then no one buys it! Anyway, I decided to take the car to the woods, burn it. No car, no problem... Since it wasn't selling... I'm so sick of it, every day is on eggshells... I'll introduce you to her. She lives a hundred kilometers away. She is very knowledgeable; I have already asked her for advice and help. She knows everything and sees everything; she is never wrong. So, yesterday I went to her and had a conversation with her. Told her about my problems with the "six", damn it. I told her, "Hey, Grandma Nina, why don't I burn that car? What am I gonna do?" You know what she says to me? "No", she says, "Sasha, don't worry. Today an angel will come to you and solve all your problems". I tell her, "What, is it really an angel?" And she tells me that it is definitely an angel! And it will get rid of the car and bring you as much money as you gave the cops! And so, I was driving away from the old woman, I was thinking all the way to my house, I looked at some girl coming to my fence, I honked at her, she turned around. An angel! Well, a pure angel!"

— Are you talking about me now, Uncle Sasha? - I laughed. – Oh, come on! I'm no angel! Uncle Sasha, you're so big, and you still believe in fairy tales! You're telling me about some old granny... It's all nonsense, a coincidence.

— No nonsense at all! It happened just like she said! You got rid of that car and gave me back exactly the money I gave the cops! You're my angel! Stay with us, you'll be a queen here! My eagles will be blowing dust off you! Do you know how much they respect you?

— Oh no, Uncle Sasha, I'm not ready...

— Well, I beg you, work with us, I'll get you any car you want, take as much money from sales as you want, all my guys are at your disposal, just don't go away forever!

Uncle Sasha spoke very sincerely.

— Okay, where's your "Moskvich-2141"? Let's go see it. Just don't tell me its story, please, I don't want to know. I'll just sell it tomorrow for you, that's all.

Before I tried to go to Mr. M.'s clinic, I was examined by almost all the doctors. I only avoided one doctor, and that was the most important one - the one who treats my Disease. Because I remember everything... I remember how all the doctors kept telling me that I had the last stage, extended duration of the disease... I remember everything, as it was the last time, several years ago, when I went to the doctors. I'm not ready to listen to this again. No, I'm not. I don't want any more death sentences; I'm not having enough fun right now.

Medicine has come a long way since then and there is now one single test, instead of a bunch of others, that accurately determines the presence and stage of my Disease. Just one test. But why are all my other tests perfect? How is that possible? I'm about to have such serious surgery, and my body is healthy! Could it be that I am cured? And the fact that the joint collapsed, is it like a residual phenomenon? I reread all the information on the Internet about my disease again. No, it is impossible to get cured. There can be remissions... but there is no way to recover permanently. It's an autoimmune disease. Your own immune system is killing you... But why the hell don't I feel it? Why do I feel healthy? Shouldn't I have painful weakness? Severe pain, after all? Why does only one hip hurt? What about my other joints? I don't take any medication. All my joints are deformed, ruined. I wonder if they hurt at all. It's hard for me to even answer this question, because I've been like this since one, practically since birth! I don't know any other life. Maybe they do hurt... Yes, that's right, ruined joints definitely hurt. But I never thought about it. There were always more pleasant images to think about. Yes... there's a wish forming in my head right now. It's growing. But for some reason I'm very afraid. More scared than ever... Yes, here it is. It's done. I'm going to go to the same hospital where I had the evil doctor lady a few years ago. I will go to the doctors who treat my Disease. Yes, I want to know what they will tell me now.

My personal diary.
June 2013

THE MOON IN THE EIGHTH HOUSE

The thought of consulting the doctor who was treating my Disease was keeping me wide awake. With every hour and every minute, my desire to get a specialist's opinion became more and more obsessive. I remembered that going to the doctor without the appropriate tests and x-rays of all my joints was pointless, so first I took all the necessary tests again, which again showed perfect results, and took x-rays of my joints. The one and most important test that would unambiguously and truthfully describe my disease and its real stage scared me. I didn't recognize myself! How could I be afraid of that! Who cares in the long run what this test will show me? I've lived somehow... I've lived so many years! And I'll live just as long, or even longer! So, I made up my mind. The test was negative! Negative! Can you imagine? My severe autoimmune disease was gone! How could that be? I did the test again. It was negative again. And again. Just to be sure. I'm healthy! How was that possible?

Are there any cases where an autoimmune disease just disappears? Even without any treatment? I also got tested for any possible autoimmune disorders. And it didn't show anything either. I am cured! It's a miracle! So, I was doing everything right in my life. I took my old medical tests and the records of that very same, disgusting doctor who had promised me a quick and painful death, and the results of the new tests and met the doctor who was treating our, although no longer my (!), illness. The male doctor was very kind to me and confirmed that I was not sick. But when I asked him how my autoimmune had "dissolved" on its own, he shook his hands and said:

— Maybe you didn't have it at all? From the beginning? The doctors back in 1978 might have made a mistake... The medicine was not that well developed, let me tell you. So, they diagnosed you with such a nightmare... And as for your ruined joints... - The doctor stopped talking and shrugged. – You know, there are all sorts of diseases that could damage your joints! You might have had something then, when you were a child, but it's gone... how else have you lived to be your age? You're perfectly healthy now.

— But, wait - I tried to get to the truth, - Forget 1978! A few years ago, they wanted to put me, by the way, in your hospital and treat me with homicidal therapy! They told me I was on my deathbed! How can you explain that? - I showed the doctor my old tests and the doctor's notes.

— These can't be your tests! They are the tests of some dying man! - the doctor said loudly and confidently, but after looking at my last name written at the top he continued, - Okay, wait... but how? Oh my God... Wow... indeed, it is our hospital...

— And you're trying to tell me that after these tests I just suddenly happened to be healthy? Can you imagine what they were going to treat me with? I wouldn't live a day! Do you have any idea what kind of treatment such terminally ill people need? - I was outraged to the core.

— There must have been some mistake... - the doctor said guiltily. – Of course, if you, in fact, had such an active disease... your joints wouldn't be the only thing... but also cirrhosis of the liver and something with the heart... no, there must be some mistake here, perhaps you have been mixed up with someone else...

— Mixed up? Really? Do you really believe that yourself? Look at what that doctor wrote! She must have been mixing me up with someone else for a long time! Look at how many notes she made! She'd examine me from head to toe! She kept telling me I was hopeless and dying!

I was overwhelmed with emotion. Those years came vividly to my mind, and I remembered every word the doctor said to me! She kept telling me that nothing could help me anymore. She insulted me, mocked me. There was always some sort of triumphant smirk on her ugly face. This sadist of a doctor genuinely savoured all the discussions about my incredibly terrible illness and about my very near death in great agony.

— She put me, not someone else, in the hospital and I was the one she wanted to give homicidal therapy to! There's no chance she mixed me up with somebody else! And all these tests? Look, there are so many of them, and all of them were done at your hospital! Isn't it too much of mixing up?

— Don't make me comment that, please? - the doctor said guiltily. - I don't know what to tell you. I really don't. I'm sorry you've been through all this. You want my advice? Forget the past. The important thing is that you're healthy now. That's all that matters. You can't prove anything to anyone now. Perhaps she had a personal grudge against you. Did you retake the tests then? No? Well, there you go... You don't have any other tests from those years. And if we imagine for a second that all this was really about you? Then you're a phenomenon. You should be very proud of yourself. No one else has ever managed to beat the disease, but you have. And by the way, that doctor hasn't worked here for three years now...

An incredible thrill overtook me. My cheeks were on fire, my heart was racing, and I couldn't stop anymore.

— Forget?! It's impossible to forget! And by the way! Why don't they let the patients in the elevator in your hospital? Why do ill people have to take the stairs instead? How is that even possible? Do you not let them in the elevator as well?

— Jesus! What is this nonsense? Calm down! How can anyone make an ill person use the stairs? You must be getting something wrong here... - The doctor was very genuinely surprised. – You know, you don't seem happy to be healthy at all!

I fell silent. I looked straight at the doctor and suddenly saw a perfectly kind human face. I was embarrassed by my behavior. And then I realized... everything that was happening was not behind looking glass! It was a normal and ordinary human life. A life, where I, a healthy person, went to see a doctor (and this sometimes happens to healthy people, too), where the doctor confirmed that I was fine and had nothing to worry about. It was like a dream, as if it had not happened to me. Of course, I was very happy to join the healthy people who are accepted and respected by society. And who are always allowed to ride the elevator.

— I'm sorry. Yes, I guess so. I'm confused... Let my sick and terrible life stay with those terrible tests. Thank you very much, doctor! You're going to write me a certificate that I'm healthy, aren't you? Will you? And will you stamp it? And a signature?

— Well, of course? It's a must!

I was happy. Here was the great joy the universe had promised me! I was healthy! I wasn't even that scared to go to surgery anymore, because I was already a healthy person going to the surgery, so of course I was sure that no doctor would ever tell me that I was on my deathbed again.

I didn't even know I was healthy when I wanted to go to the hospital to see Mr. M. How fate took me!

I called Mr. G. and told him that I was healthy and that I had a certificate to that effect. The surgeon, after congratulating me, said:

— Lena, I am very happy for you. I already called Mr. B., but I told him about your diagnosis and the endoprosthesis surgery. So, you'll have to tell him later that you don't have that diagnosis. Call him now, and he will schedule an appointment for you; You'll have to bring your test results and do a checkup with him.

I was happy. I dialed Mr. B., said hello, and introduced myself. I really enjoyed my status, new for both myself and for all the people around me; the status of a healthy person.

Mr. B. made an appointment for me in his office tomorrow.

— Could you tell me the address, please? - I asked.

— You can find the address on the Internet! - The head of the traumatology department answered rudely and sharply.

It was like I was back in that sick reality of mine. That's exactly how doctors talked to patients, like me! And this one was no exception! He didn't know that I was already healthy...

— Well, okay, I'll look... - I continued the conversation. – Could you tell me your office number? And the floor?

— Ask somebody! I'm the toughest guy here, everybody knows me! I don't have time to talk to you. I'm actually working!

After a short and unpleasant conversation with Mr. B., I wondered... Why so? After all, my surgeon informed him about me, a patient, who is about to undergo such a difficult operation, and, therefore, most likely, this patient is disabled and is moving around in a wheelchair or on crutches, as it is already time to replace my joint... Well, is it really so difficult to tell the address of the clinic? Name the street? This clinic has several buildings, and how do you want a person with a damaged musculoskeletal system to wander around and look for the traumatology building there? The rudeness and clear sarcastic superiority of the doctor over the patient was astounding. I started looking online for information about him and I found it! The doctor was about forty years old, was a solidly built man, and looked more like an impudent and fat bribe-taking traffic cop than a doctor. A few years ago, we, the drivers of our titanic homeland, encountered such unpleasant characters often and everywhere on all the roads. Having searched on the Internet, I found some compromising information on the doctor. It turned out that not so long ago he was on trial. There was a lot of money involved in the case.

— Well, thank God I'll only be staying in his ward, and I'll still have my surgeon to do the surgery - I exhaled.

Again, I looked very well, and it was impossible to tell by looking at me that I was in need of major surgery. I got behind the wheel of my car and drove to the doctor's appointment. Before the trip, I called my surgeon and just in case, asked him what he had said about me to Mr. B. My surgeon replied that he only named the diagnosis and the surgery that the patient, i.e. me, needed. That was it. So now for sure, Mr. B. had no excuse. He thought he was talking to a very sick person who couldn't move around on his own and was feeling very unwell. And, of course, he was absolutely certain that today he was meeting with exactly the kind of severe patient who would probably be brought to him for an appointment...

The whole of Moscow was stuck in a terrible traffic jam. I never liked to be late, so I left much earlier. But nevertheless, I knew that I had a chance of being late and not arriving at the appointed time. I called Mr. B. and warned him when I was just a short distance from the hospital:

— Good afternoon, I'm almost there, but I'm afraid I might be five minutes late while I look for your office!

— I'm not waiting a minute! - the doctor answered harshly and, as always, rudely. - I have to leave! So either don't be late, or come back tomorrow.

— Just wait five minutes, please! It took me four hours to get here! - I was very indignant.

— You think you're special, huh? I have patients waiting for me in another clinic! That's it! Don't be late tomorrow!

The conversation was over. I cursed loudly. Why would you make an appointment for me if you had to leave anyway? What kind of a joke is this? I drove to the clinic and parked, hoping the doctor hadn't left yet. I was, as I said, five minutes late. Suddenly I saw him, in person, walking out of the building. If I had arrived a minute later, I would have missed him. But as it was, I could tell I caught him right outside the clinic. Fat and clumsy, the doctor slowly and awkwardly was going down the steps. I got out of the car. The doctor noticed me, stopped, smiled broadly, and said coquettishly;

— Oh! What beautiful girls we have here! Young lady! Aren't you here for me by any chance?

The situation, I'm telling you, was very amusing! Mr. B. stood in front of me, smiling lusciously, wiggling his torso from side to side, like little girls do in their mothers' outfits in front of the mirror, he obviously wanted to make the nicest impression on me.

— I am, by chance! - I answered very seriously.
— I'm from Mr. G., for an endoprosthesis surgery. It was me you had an appointment with, I was the one who called you.

You should have seen his reaction!

— How?! Is that you?! It can't be... You're so beautiful! How can you have any pains? Oh... What are we standing here for?! Let's go quickly to my office! We need to discuss everything with you! - Mr. B. forgot all about his other meetings.

— Come in, please! - The kind doctor was very nice. Opening the door of his office, he gestured for me to come in first, "Please, make yourself comfortable! Would you like some coffee? Tea, perhaps?

— No, thank you...

— Oh, my God! You're in heels, too! Why do you need this operation? Don't do it, please! It doesn't make any sense that you need this operation. It just can't be!

— I, - Mr. B. pronounced the word "I" with great respect and expression, - am the whole head of traumatology - the doctor said loudly and almost in syllables, probably to make it more convincing. - I never would have noticed anything wrong with you! And I'm a professional! Don't do the operation! I'm begging you. It's a very difficult operation. You may never be able to get up again.

Mr. B. was genuinely worried about me.

— I'll be fine, I know it. Don't you worry!

— Maybe I can talk you out of it. You're so gorgeous... - The doctor looked at me with admiration mixed with sadness, and now he was really compassionate, as a doctor should be.

— No, I'm doing the surgery, it's decided. Don't worry, I've already done one... As you can see, everything is fine...

— Well, then I'll give you the best room... - Mr. B. fussed. - What else can I do for you? Well... Well...

— Can I smoke in the room? - I smiled now.

— Lenochka! Anything for you! Of course, you can smoke! Just open the window, okay? Because we have a law now! Smoking is forbidden. But you can do anything! And don't worry, please! I'll do everything I can, I'll provide everything. I'm actually on vacation starting next week, and I'm supposed to leave... but I'll stay until you have the operation!

— That won't be necessary! Go, please! You certainly should! – Great, just what I "needed"!

— No, no! I've made up my mind! I can't rest easy knowing that you have such a difficult operation! And don't even try to convince me otherwise!

A fat middle-aged doctor fluttered in front of me like a young butterfly.

— I'll give you the best doctor! Just remember: he has a wife and a small child! - Mr. B. obviously didn't want to share me with anyone.

— Okay, I'll keep that in mind, - I smiled. - How much do I owe you for all this?

Mr. B. raised his eyebrows upward in surprise:

— Lenochka! I'm not in it for the money! Please don't think of me like that! What money? Please, don't offend me with money anymore! I just want you to be happy!

Looking ahead, I want to say that Mr. B. was probably "offended" later, after all, because he took the money.

When I got home, I opened my astrological forecast, as usual. I knew it by heart, of course, but the very picture of the planets on the ecliptic had a calming effect on me, giving me the illusion of control over the situation.

— Well? What do the stars say? - my husband asked.

— We won't have to run away from this hospital, will we?

— No, this time I'm getting an endoprosthesis.

— But will the operation be successful? Will it be okay? - my husband got worried.

— Of course - I answered. - But not right away.

— Are you going to be in a lot of pain?

— A lot, yeah. And also I'm scared. Very. You know, I'm a big coward... You know how scared I get...

— Honestly, I don't know how you do it all... - said my husband. - I just can't get my head around it... You're not a coward, you're very strong. And I'm so proud of you. So many trials in your life... I would have died a long time ago. And you're doing such an amazing job... You should write a book.

— I have the moon in the eighth house, - I said thoughtfully. - The moon is our soul... Can you imagine how my poor soul suffers in a house of death? If you only knew how I don't want to relive it all! The terrible pain, the disgusting attitude of the medical staff... I have to learn to walk again... it's all so hard! And this is not my last surgery... there will be others...

— Is your soul always-always suffering? Without stopping at all? - The husband seemed agitated.

— No, of course, only on the accompanying difficult aspects, - I smiled, - It's not all that bad! Sometimes my soul's just crazy high! We'll get through this!

The day of my hospitalization came. The hospital where Mr. B. worked and where my surgeon was to perform my complicated operation was in a squalid and dilapidated state. The hospital in which Mr. B. worked, in which my surgeon was to perform my complicated operation, was in a squalid and dilapidated state. The walls were shabby and painted, the ceilings monstrous, the plaster crumbling, and the floors disgusting and dirty. This hospital was simply the epitome of unhygienic.

— Hello, where can I get my shoe covers? - I asked the security guard at the hospital entrance.

— What shoe covers? What am I, a shoe store? So go! We don't have any shoe covers!

A freight elevator on the first floor swung open, and two nurses rolled out a gurney with a bleeding man on it. The unfortunate man was lying unclothed, covered by a sheet. And, it seemed to me, he was under anesthesia. The nurses wheeled the patient with the open wounds down the dusty corridor, occasionally bumping the gurney against the usual hospital visitors. The visitors, wearing dirty shoes and outerwear, recoiled and cringed squeamishly.

— Oh my God... - I said quietly to myself, - Tomorrow I will be in his place

It's not a hospital, it's a barn! - my husband was indignant. - A man is covered in blood! And there's such a dump all around... Everything is supposed to be sterile here! What a disregard for people!

We went up to the trauma floor and immediately met Mr. B. When he saw me, he smiled coquettishly and exclaimed in a lusciously sweet voice:

— Lenochka! - he opened his arms wide, as if in front of an impending embrace. - I've been waiting for you!

But when he saw my companion next to me, he immediately wiped the smile off his face and took on a haughty look:

— Who the hell are you? - He turned to my husband in a very dismissive manner.

— Husband.

— That's my husband, - I confirmed.

— No, that won't do! - Mr. B. said, - We don't need a husband here! We'll get you out of here ourselves! Let the husband go!

At the same moment Mr. B.'s phone rang. He answered it. And, without paying any attention to us and leaving us at a complete loss, Mr. B. quickly left.

— Well, what are we going to do? Won't they let me in? - My husband was very indignant.

— Everything will be alright. Just don't say anything. Don't argue with him. Don't make it worse - my heart raced. – He promised me the best room. At least let him keep his promise! Look how miserable it is around here... Tomorrow I have a very complicated surgery. I don't want to think about anything but that everything will be alright. I don't want Mr. B. to take revenge on me for his unjustified fantasies about me and his wounded ego.

— I'd like to punch him in the face, - his husband hissed.

— Don't. Stop it. The main thing now is to survive the operation without any major losses.

The procedure of my hospitalization in this hospital was very difficult and long, but I overcame all the difficulties. I was really assigned the best room, as promised. The best room was a small room with two beds, the walls of which were very shabby and painted, apparently by former patients. Under the ceiling hung an air conditioner with a short cut wire sticking out to the side. A definite plus was the toilet, which was located right outside the door of the "best" room.

The door of the room swung open, and Mr. B., my attending physician assigned to me, walked in. Dr. I. was a young man, about thirty-three years of age, and gave the impression of an extremely insecure man, though rather handsome. He was small in stature and always looked straight at his feet when talking, as if he was very embarrassed. Uncertain Dr.

I flipped through my card, which I was given at the hospital, noted that my tests were excellent and that I had absolutely nothing to fear, since I was going to surgery as a completely healthy person and my body was completely normal. I felt a great relief. I don't often hear from a man in a white coat that everything is going to be okay!

Evening came, and visiting hours were over. My husband went home. And now I was waiting for him only in a day, or even two, because tomorrow was a crucial day, the day of my surgery, after which I had to spend a day in the intensive care unit.

I was very nervous. I understood that I needed to sleep, because early in the morning I would be taken to the operating room, but there was no sleep. There was only fear, melancholy and a feeling of complete doom. I came out of the room, I went to the nurse on duty:

— Good evening, do you have any sleeping pills? I'd like to sleep, because tomorrow is the surgery... I'm very scared...

— We have it, - the pretty and friendly nurse told me. - But I don't know if I can give it to you. You have such a difficult operation tomorrow! Won't you and I hurt ourselves with this pill?

— What am I going to do? I feel like I'll go crazy before morning if I don't fall asleep!

— So... - The nurse on duty was thinking. - What should we do with you? You just understand me, please - she went on, - I would give you this pill, I'm not sorry, but I'm very worried that it would not cause you any harm!

— I understand, - I said, and instantly I felt great sympathy for this girl. It was so unusual and nice for me to have someone in a hospital, in a white coat, taking care of my health.

— I've got it! - The nurse exclaimed cheerfully, - Mr. B. hasn't gone home yet! It's so strange... he never stays out late. It's the first time this has happened to him! He's in charge, he knows exactly what you can and can't do! There's his office, see? Can you go over there and ask him? Cause I can't leave my post...

— Of course, thank you, - I smiled at the pretty girl. I wandered toward Mr. B.'s office and was very worried. The last time I had seen him was when his phone rang and he unceremoniously left my husband and me in utter bewilderment. I felt that after he saw my spouse, his attitude toward me had changed dramatically. I was anticipating his boorish, arrogant, spitting tone again, just as he had the first time we had spoken. My intuition had not failed me.

When I knocked and opened the door to the office of the head of traumatology, I saw Mr. B. He was sitting at his desk, clearly bored. It was obvious that he had finished his work long ago.

— Well, come in, why are you standing at the door? Don't be shy! - Mr. B. called me rudely and with a smirk, switching to first-name with me. I went in and sat down on the low sofa next to his desk.

Well? What's up? - The fat doctor theatrically and awkwardly threw his legs on the table so that the soles of his shoes were almost near my face. - Did you miss me?

Mr. B. tried his best to give the impression of a brutal and self-assured alpha male. I moved away from the soles of his shoes.

I came to see if I could take sleeping pills. After all, I have an operation tomorrow... The nurse sent me to ask you... She's afraid to give me a pill herself...

— He's right to be afraid. Everyone here is afraid of me! - The arrogant and cocky doctor moved his fat legs off the table. - Do you know why I am sitting here? - Pointing to his chair with both hands, Mr. B. asked me.

— Where? In your office? - I didn't understand the question.

— Yes, in the goddamn office! Do you think I want to sit here? I'm on vacation! I'm not even supposed to be here! And I'm sitting here like an idiot! - The doctor was emotionally disturbed, and I already knew what he was getting at.

— I've been waiting all night for you to come to me, - Mr. B continued. His tone changed, I would say, to condescendingly affectionate, as if he was giving me a chance to earn his affection once again. - I like you very much... Very much... Haven't you realized that yet? Shall we have some cognac? - At this phrase he jumped in his chair, as if he had had some kind of epiphany.

— You what? What cognac? I have an operation early in the morning! I can't! - I protested.

— Just a little bit, just for the mood! Come on, come on, please! - I was being persuaded by the unreasonable doctor.

— Oh, really?! No, of course not. I don't drink at all...

— No problem, - an emotional Mr. B. interrupted me, - if you don't want some cognac, let's have some whiskey! I've got whiskey!

I got really scared. The situation was disgusting. The head of traumatology at a well-known Moscow hospital did not care at all what happened to a patient in his department tomorrow during an operation of the highest degree of complexity! He needed me today and now! Right here in his office on this couch, or maybe on his desk. He purposely didn't go on his vacation, came to work and stayed late, gave me the best room... for all this he craved immediate compensation right there in his office! He even got me drunk on alcohol, which was completely out of my head! All means are good in war! Who cares what happens to me tomorrow? It is necessary to get everything out of me today, while I am beautiful, sad and scared to death, the upcoming difficult surgery to replace the hip joint. There he is to comfort me!

— No, no, - I shook my head. - I can't, I'm sorry...

Well, stop breaking down! - Mr. B. sat down next to me on the couch. - We're just a little bit, it won't affect your operation, I'm a doctor, I know...

The office door swung open abruptly. Mr. B. instantly jumped away from me like a scalded man.

A young, slender woman, in her thirties, with petite and angry features, entered the office. The woman wore a white robe and was holding large cardboard bags, from which the clinking of bottles could be heard. They were probably "thank-yous" from patients.

— Well, well! - she said with importance, loudness and expression.

— It's a patient, she came to ask me something... - explained Mr. B. to the woman. And turning to me, he said again in his spiteful tone:

— So, what was it you wanted to ask me? Sleeping pills? No, you can't. You have surgery early in the morning, go to your room! And by the way, here's your anesthesiologist," he smiled at the word "anesthesiologist" and pointed to a lady in a white coat. - Now go to your room.

I cannot tell you, my dear readers, in words what was going on in my soul. It was a complete nightmare. It was obvious that the anesthesiologist was the mistress

THE MOON IN THE EIGHTH HOUSE

of Mr. B. And the picture she saw in the head's office was unambiguously interpreted in her own way. I made myself an enemy, on which tomorrow's operation will depend. I was afraid to even think about it. At a loss, I called my family and my best friend and told them the details of what had happened. I wanted them to know what had happened the day before if something happened to me during the operation tomorrow. In the meantime my anesthesiologist came into my room. She was holding some sheets of paper with text printed on them.

— Read it and sign it, - she said very strictly and coldly.

— What is it? - I asked.

— Anesthesia risks. It's all there, - the doctor answered haughtily and stared at the wall.

I began to read. There were several anesthesia risks on the sheets of paper, namely, how the patient was expected to survive the anesthesia. But the risk that had a check mark next to it, the risk that my anesthesiologist had identified for me, shocked me. It said that the patient, i.e. me, would die within a day, regardless of the surgery!

— What's that? - I was still hoping it was some kind of mistake. - Am I the one who is going to die within 24 hours?

— Sign it quickly! I don't have time to deal with you here! My workday is long over! - said the doctor loudly in an icy voice.

— How can I sign this? Why do you need it? I'm healthy! All my tests are perfect! I've gone through all the doctors!

— I don't give a damn about your tests! You're like a star to me! - The sadistic woman in the white coat went on a rampage. - I'm sick and tired of these problems! The other day we had one just like you, with the same operation. So now she will never walk, her sciatic nerve was damaged! And who to blame it on? Me, of course! I did the epidural wrong! No, that's enough! Either you sign, or I refuse to do the anesthesia! Otherwise, they'll screw something up for you, and I'll have to answer for it. Besides, your joints are all crooked, which means your spine's crooked too. That's why I can inject you in the wrong place, and you'll be bedridden, you won't even be able to sit up! Sign it quickly!

— I have a straight spine, - I tried to argue with the sadistic woman, but suddenly I felt very weak, my head was spinning, and I realized that I simply had no strength left to resist.

— I don't care what kind of spine you have, the fact is, anything can happen to you in surgery, and I'm not going to answer.

— Can you give me two minutes? I need to make a phone call...

— Two minutes, - the doctor said with emphasis on the word "two," and left the room.

— I called my surgeon. Very quickly and in two words I told him everything that had happened and what the anesthesiologist wanted from me.

— Should I offer her some money? - I asked my surgeon.

— Try to suggest it, - he agreed. - But you have to understand, I don't have any more hospitals to operate on you. I'm already set up for tomorrow. She's normal as a doctor, she's just jealous... Don't listen to her, don't be afraid, everything will be fine. Len, let's go to sleep now, the operation is tomorrow... I need to get some sleep... I need to rest...

An anesthesiologist came into the room.

— Well? Will you sign it?

— I'm sorry...maybe money will solve our problem?

— What money?! - The doctor hissed at me. - Do you know where to shove it? All right, that's it! You don't seem to understand anything... that's it, you're not going to have an operation! - And sharply, turning to the door, she resolutely and quickly left the room.

— Wait a minute! - I shouted after her.

After a few seconds, the triumphant anesthesiologist returned to the room and haughtily, with a sarcastic smile, handed me a paper and pen:

— Sign it!

I signed. I signed a medical document that said I would die within 24 hours, regardless of the surgery.

LIBERATION

When I woke up, I felt an unbearable pain in my leg. I wanted to call someone, but my voice was gone for some reason. I could only make a faint sound, like a mouse squeaking. I tried to raise my head, to move somehow to draw the attention of the women in white coats who were in the intensive care unit, but I was very nauseous and dizzy, so all these attempts were in vain. The nurses were walking around the ICU between the beds with patients, but they did not look in my direction. I didn't give up trying to draw their attention to myself. I continued to push my body up a little and make squeaking noises. The pain in my leg was becoming less and less bearable. I jerked my head and lifted it off the pillow, but right at that moment I threw up right on myself. One of the women in white coats in the ICU looked right at me. She held her gaze on me for a few seconds. In that time, I tried to call her with my facial expressions and my squeaking. The woman turned away and walked over to the bed with the patient opposite from me. Tears rolled down my face from excruciating pain and complete hopelessness, but I still kept trying to get somebody's attention. Nothing worked. The medics left the ICU.

I don't remember how much time I spent in that deepest layer of hell, in that creepy capital city hospital in the ICU, but it seemed like an eternity to me. My voice was eventually back, and when some of the people in white coats came into the ICU again, I could call out loud enough. I begged, "Please, help me... please..."

But no one came to rescue me! No one. People in white coats didn't even turn their heads in my direction. In the meantime, I was vomiting profusely, and my pain was growing. I was groaning non-stop, and one of the patients could not stand it any longer and turned to the doctors,

— Get over to that woman, she's sick! She's always groaning, she won't let me sleep!

I heard a woman's voice clearly in response:

— Do not approach her! It is prohibited!

I heard that phrase very clearly, it was not an auditory hallucination caused by the wild pain. Someone, and I even knew exactly who, had forbidden me to get help! I tried to stop groaning so as not to disturb the patients, tried to switch off from the pain, to sink into sleep, but it did not work. Realizing that no one would help me here, I nevertheless tried again and again to get through to the doctors. I very much hoped that some person would come into the ICU, even accidentally, who had not been warned that I could not be helped.

— Please... come here... I need help... please - I repeated these words like a mantra, but it was in vain. Probably everyone had been warned.

The next day I was transferred to my room. I came out of the anesthesia and felt much better. My husband was already beside me. I told him about the conversation I had with my surgeon in the corridor before the surgery, about the painful antibiotic shot they gave me, and about the terrible and humiliating procedure of epidural anesthesia, when my anesthesiologist yelled at me in a very rude, boorish way,

— Keep your back straight! I said straight! Or I'll give you the wrong injection, and you'll never stand up again! Sit up straight, I said! Don't you dare twitch or squeak at me! I'll cripple you!

A nurse came into the room.

— A bandage! - he said loudly, looking at me. The talkative nurse treating my wound said:

— What golden hands our Dr. I. has! What a good stitch he did for you! I can't help it!

— I'm very happy that I'm doing so well there, that's great, - I said, smiling and making conversation. - But I'm sorry, what does this have to do with your Dr. I.? My surgeon, Mr. G., operated on me.

— No, he didn't! - The nurse was very surprised. - You were operated on by Dr. I.! This is his first operation of such difficulty! Didn't you know? His whole department is congratulating him!

— Wait! What are you saying? This can't be happening! My surgeon operated on me! He operated on my left leg a few years ago, and now my right leg...

— Who's your surgeon? You nust have mixed something up! There were no other surgeons here. You were operated on by our Dr. I.! He told everyone himself about it in the resident's room! And how difficult the operation was, and even how you woke up while he was stitching you up...

It was true that I woke up. For a while the anesthesia just stopped working. At that time, Mr. G. was stitching up my wound. I screamed violently in insane pain. But seconds later I fell back into oblivion, and I don't remember anything else. Of course, I'm not a doctor, so it's hard to say what helped me to feel the entire vivid spectrum of the unbearable pain I had to endure on the operating table. Either my body came out of the anesthesia on its own there, during the surgery, or it was helped to do so - remains a mystery.

— What do you mean there were no other surgeons? I personally talked to Mr. G. before the operation, he came here to your hospital specifically to operate on me!

— I don't know what you're talking about, - the nurse shrugged. - I don't know anything about it. Maybe you were dreaming about it.

I called Mr. G., and he didn't answer. How could that be? This can't be happening! I would never trust Dr. Y. to operate on me. Did my surgeon really let Dr.Y. replace my joint? And what's standing there now? Will I ever be able to walk again?

My husband called a nurse into the room.

— Do you know who operated on me? - I asked her a question.

— Of course! - the nurse smiled. - Our wonderful Dr. I.!

— No! - I was utterly perplexed. - Mr. G. operated on me! He came to your hospital specifically for the operation!

— No, no one came here! If someone had come here, I would have known for sure! - the nurse was surprised. - The operation was performed by Dr. I.!

— I don't know who told you such nonsense, - I began to say.

— That's what Dr. I. said! Why bullshit? We all congratulated him, he told us how difficult the surgery was! Don't worry, it's the first time he's ever had such an operation, but it worked!

— Please, call Dr. Y. to me, - I asked. - I want to ask him personally!

— He's already gone home, he's not in the hospital. Now it's only tomorrow.

— How come he left without even coming to see me? The last time I saw him, by the way, was before the operation. Isn't he my doctor?

— Well, why do you need him now? Let him go home and rest. Can't we handle you ourselves? We know what to do! - The nurse shook her hands and went out of the room.

I lay there and wondered... how could it be? Why hadn't anyone seen my surgeon? We were sitting in the hallway talking to him, not hiding from anyone. I'm not crazy yet, am I? Mr. G., is he an invisible surgeon?

I asked my husband to go out into the corridor to the other nurses and ask them if they knew about the details of my surgery. I had no doubts about my surgeon. I knew for a fact that he couldn't spit on me and give me to some Dr. I. who had never done this kind of surgery in his life. It just did not fit in my head. My surgeon is a very responsible person, he would never do that. But I was outraged by the fact that Dr. I lied so brazenly! He decided to take the credit for my surgeon! The thirst for justice is very strong in me from the beginning, because of my Ascendant in Aquarius.

Everyone is just saying that you had the surgery performed by Dr. I. Even the patients of the trauma department! Turns out everyone knows! This hospital has never performed such a complicated surgery before, you're the first... The whole floor is discussing you and Dr. I! They say he's good, he operated on you well, - my husband told me.

— Did you tell them that my surgeon operated on me, not Dr. Y.?

— I tried, but they asked me not to talk nonsense... Len... maybe it's true? Maybe Dr. I. operated on you after all.

— No! - I exclaimed. - No! What are you?! Don't even doubt it! They're all lying. I don't know if it was Dr. Y. who convinced them all to believe it, or if they're all lying for some reason, but they're definitely lying!

Suddenly, probably by mistake, the nurse who was giving me the antibiotic shot looked into the room. She called me into the room just as we were sitting in the corridor with Mr. G. and talking. That is, she saw him unequivocally.

— Young lady! - I called out to the nurse. - You were the one who gave me the antibiotic, right?

The nurse nodded.

— But do you know who operated on me? - I asked.

— Dr. I.! - without thinking, she answered.

— But you saw my surgeon, didn't you? We were sitting in the hallway together, weren't we?! Do you remember? - I was very surprised.

— No, I didn't see anybody. There was no one there but you in the hallway!

The nurse left.

— And this one's lying. She saw Mr. G. Do they make me out to be crazy? - I tried to find a motive for such collective lies. - Why would they do that?

In the meantime, my health deteriorated, and my husband stayed the night with me, in my room. No one else entered the room at all. A couple of times, very quickly, I smoked. I was worried that someone would come and there would be trouble, but it didn't happen. The next morning I got through to my surgeon and asked him about the surgery. He told me in detail how it went, how and what he did. I asked if Dr. I was there. Mr. G. replied that he had come in, but was not present. I didn't feel well. A nurse came in. That nice, sweet girl who was afraid to give me a pill before the surgery, so as not to hurt me.

— How are you feeling? It's my shift today, so if you need anything, tell me! - The nurse smiled her charming smile.

— Thank you. I don't feel very good, to be honest...

The nurse got sad:

— Don't worry about it. You should be... it's only been a day after such a complicated surgery! Has your doctor been to see you yet?

— No, he didn't! Can you get him for me?

— Yes, of course! - the girl smiled again. - I'll get you!

A few minutes later, a nurse looked into our room:

— He's a little busy right now, he said he'd be here in about fifteen minutes!

Two hours passed. Dr. I. did not come.

— Go, please, - I said to my husband - find him! Tell him to come. Doesn't he care whether his patient is alive or not?

A few minutes later the spouse came in alone:

— I found him, but he said he'd be here in about twenty minutes, he had a complicated patient.

— Well, let's wait... - I exhaled. - Although to be honest, I don't feel very good... I wish I could talk to a doctor... Maybe I need a shot or a pill...

The nurse from yesterday came in to treat the wound. Husband went to the nearest store to buy something tasty for dinner.

— When I told Dr. I. about your imaginary surgeon, he was very surprised! He thought that the anesthesia had done something to you - he said, wiping the antiseptic on my stitches.

— Look, I was just wondering, - the insolence and deceit of my doctor was astounding, - were you working on the day of my surgery?

— No, it wasn't my shift, why?

— It's nothing! I just want to know, are you deliberately lying to me now, knowing the whole truth, or have you been convinced that everything was as Dr. I. says?!

— I'm not lying, - the nurse took offense. - I wasn't here at all, and I'm taking Dr. Y's word for it. And anyway, that's all anyone ever talks about.

— Well, if you weren't here at all, then why are you telling me so confidently that you were lied to? Would you vouch for all these people? Are you willing to sign for them? Are you really that gullible?! Did I go to a mental hospital or something? There's nothing wrong with my head, in case you haven't noticed! So why don't you listen to me, a patient in your department? I've told you a hundred times and I'll tell you again that my surgeon, Mr. G., operated on me - I said loudly, in my convincing, clear voice.

— Well, then why does everyone lie? What do they do it for? - It was obvious that the nurse doubted his former beliefs and, moving away from my wound, looked at me with a trusting look.

— I don't know what they need it for yet, - I shrugged.

— Is it possible that Dr. I. decided to put a price on himself, at the expense of your surgeon! As if he was so tough, he operated on such a difficult patient... he performed such a difficult operation...

— Well, as an option, - I agreed. - Although I'm not a complicated patient, I had all the tests perfect and the conclusions of all the doctors...

— Yeah? - the nurse was very surprised. - It's a strange thing...

— What's strange about it? - I didn't understand.

— Well, actually, everyone says that you have a very severe diagnosis, and you were at death's door...

— Oh, come on! - I exclaimed in surprise. - I'm dying! I came to your hospital in full dress and high heels! Now I'm lying there barely alive... And by the way, your head of traumatology repeatedly told me that he never would have thought that I could have any pain at all!

THE MOON IN THE EIGHTH HOUSE

— You don't look like a dying man now - smiled the nurse. - Well, the head of our department is now warming up in the south...

— Did he leave? When did he go?

— Yes, two days ago... - the nurse was thinking. - You know what... Our Dr. I. would not dare to tell such a big lie by himself... he's not the type... He's too shy... But by the order of Mr. B. - he could definitely do it! He obeys him in everything. They always go together...

— Exactly! - I picked up on the nurse's thought. – I got it! They had a document that the anesthesiologist had beaten out of me, and it said that I would die within 24 hours! It all made sense! - my hunch was making a very clear cause-and-effect connection. - And of course, they decided not to miss such a great opportunity to publicize their miserable department and pass me off as a terminally ill person, whom they, benefactors, saved, and still have such a complicated operation! What a clown! Exactly, it was Mr. B. who planned the whole thing and took off on vacation, leaving Dr. I. to take the rap!

— It looks like it! - my ally rejoiced at our deductions.

— But, please, don't tell on me, so no one knows what we were talking about here," the nurse worried.

— Look, don't be afraid! I won't turn you in, but I intend to get to the truth. First of all, your doctors are, to put it mildly, very dishonest people! And secondly, I will not allow them to assert themselves at the expense of my surgeon! Besides, I don't want people to turn to them for help after they lie, thinking that they are so good at pulling patients out of the grave!

— That's as much as you want, just don't give me away...

— Don't worry, - I interrupted the nurse. The puzzle that had settled in my head kept adding up. - Now it makes perfect sense to me why Dr. Y. doesn't come to me! And he won't! So it's useless for me to wait for him... I don't think I'll see him again. Of course he doesn't want any questions from me! That's crazy! Just like that, abandoning his patient after surgery!

— No, - the nurse shook his head. - He can't come to you. He's your attending. And besides, he has to do the discharge papers... he has to look at you... So you have to see him anyway.

— I won't see him, I'm telling you! Look at me? I don't think so! He wants more than anything in the world to never see me now! Probably because I am now the greatest threat to his reputation, he hates me. So does Mr. B. By the way - I said to the nurse, "there are some cigarettes in the nightstand. Could you hand them over, please?

— What do you need it for? - My ally looked at me incredulously.

— I want a smoke! - I answered persuasively.

— You can't do that here... Especially in a ward...

— Oh, come on! Your hospital is a model of lawlessness! And besides, I got permission from the superintendent himself. I'm serious!

The nurse hesitated for a second.

— Do you smoke? - I asked him.

— Yes...

— Then you can smoke, too. Don't be afraid! First of all, no one will come here but my husband. And secondly, Mr. B. really gave me permission. And thirdly, your doctors screwed up so badly and lied so badly that no one will say a word! They all want me to go home, and they want to forget about my hospitalization as if it were a bad dream! I guarantee it! Give me a cigarette, after all!

After my solemn speech, the nurse promptly complied with my demands.

— Then I, too... may I? - He asked tentatively, but quite contentedly.

— Of course! Smoke to your heart's content! And if anything, you can blame it all on me! - I smiled. – I smiled. "I forced and coerced you," I said.

Lighting a cigarette and looking at her, I added:

— I'm going to get out of this hospital and quit this crap for good!

We smoked with my ally, and he went on to work. My husband came back:

— There's smoke coming from the hallway! - he said fearfully. - They're going to evict us!

— No one will evict me, don't worry! - I told my husband about my conversation with the nurse.

— Wow! - said my dumbfounded husband. - I'm going to go and see Dr. Y. again! I'll see if he's going to visit you! Because his promised twenty minutes are long gone!

— Go, - I agreed. - I wondered how he'd get out of it this time. Tell him I don't feel well. That's true. And please call the nurse for me, see if I need a shot...

The husband nodded and left the room. A minute later a smiling nurse entered, but immediately she stopped smiling and asked excitedly:

— Were you smoking in the room?

— Yes, - I replied nonchalantly. - The supervisor gave me permission.

— Really? - the nurse said incredulously. - He chastises us a lot for smoking... we run out into the street to smoke... He's very strict about it!

— I offered to smoke if you want - I said to the girl - It's smoky in here anyway! And me, by the way, give me a cigarette, I'll keep you company!

— No way! We can't! What if someone comes in? - the nurse got worried.

— Who should go in?

— Your attending doctor Y. - answered the girl. - He'll kill me and be sure to tell Mr. B. everything when he comes back from vacation.

— I can assure you that your Dr. Y. will definitely not come here. And if such a miracle happens, I promise you that he will never tell anyone anything! I've got dirt on your Dr. I. and a lot of questions for him! Smoke, don't be afraid!

The nurse opened the door of the room and looked out into the corridor. There was no one in the hallway.

— All right, let's make it quick while no one's around! It's smoky in here anyway...- She handed me a cigarette and lit hers. - What's your dirt?

And I told the nice girl about everything. And about what had happened in this hospital with me before the operation, and about the intensive care, and about the fact that I was operated by Mr. G., and not by Dr. I. in any way.

The nurse listened to me with great interest. Her eyes sparkled.

— That's why I really want you - I continued, - to tell everyone that it was my surgeon who operated on me, and no one else. All those who have been misled. Because, for example, the girl who injected me with antibiotics before my surgery is lying. She knows the truth, but she's lying, she's with them.

— This is a nightmare, - said the nurse, dazed but pleased and excited by this exciting information. - I can't believe what you've told me! Of course, I've seen a lot of things here, but this... Yes, that anesthesiologist is always so arrogant... I can't stand her... and our chief seems to be afraid of her! The ICU is her realm, of course they're afraid to go near you if she's forbidden it! What a bastard! She's gone completely crazy with her Mr. B.!

— Will you give me some kind of pain relief shot? - I asked the nurse.

— Of course!

The nurse gave me a shot.

— Can I still come over for a smoke and a chat? - She smiled at me with her charming smile.

— Of course you can come! The nurse left.

The door of the room swung open, and a very excited husband ran in:

— He's gone home! - he exclaimed. - Can you imagine?! Dr. I. ran away! What a bastard!

— Well, that's what I had to prove - I said calmly. - I'm not going to be able to do that - I said, and then I was gone.

— It's so smoky in here, - my husband said with a sniff. - I think I'll smoke, too. I feel like smoking...

— Yeah, sure! We're allowed to do anything around here now! Let somebody try to say something!

There was a knock at the door of the room.

— May I? - When he opened the door, a young guy poked his curly head into our room.

— Come in, - I said.

The guy was about twenty-seven years old. He was a patient in the trauma unit, and, as he told us later, in a few days he was going to undergo a series of complicated surgeries on his shoulder.

— Is that your smoking? - The guy asked.

— We do, - I nodded.

— Can I have one, too? - The guy pulled out a cigarette from behind his ear.

— You may, come in, sit down!

The guy's name was Petya. He went to the hospital after a car accident in which he was badly hurt. But by now he was feeling much better. Petya, like all the inhabitants of the traumatology department, had heard about my operation and about the glorious hero Dr. I. My husband and I began to tell him the truth. Petya was shocked.

A nurse I already knew knocked on the door of the room.

— May I join you? - he said, almost in a whisper and conspiratorially.

— Come on in! - I smiled. - We're not the only ones here anymore!

I'm having a smoke...

I got it, smoke it!

And we all went up in smoke together, for company.

By evening, all the smoking patients, as well as the nurses in the trauma department, knew that "we had smokers," and one by one, or two or three by three, came to our room. We welcomed everyone and told them all the truth about my surgery. The numerous visitors to our room listened with bated breath to my husband and me. The nurses and patients alike were completely on my side and took everything I said without the slightest doubt. No one doubted that Dr. Y was not involved in my operation.

My ward turned into a real passageway, and I became a thought leader and reformer. People came to me all the time. Some smoked, some just talked or listened to me. Everyone wanted to know some more interesting and juicy details. There was always a flow of people. When I wanted to sleep, my husband would gather the crowd in the corridor and tell them that from that time on no one was allowed to come in and knock on our door. The reformer was resting. My associates understood everything and never broke our rules. I became a real star of traumatology!

The next day I was in severe pain again, and my husband decided by all means to bring me the attending physician.

— I don't trust him anymore, so I'll walk beside him, he won't fool me now! - said my spouse. - I'll bring him for sure!

— Please come back soon - I moaned. - I don't feel so good, I'm afraid to be alone...

— Yes, I'll be quick! I'll get the nurse to come and give you a shot, maybe? - my husband got nervous.

— Maybe, yes, call her.

My husband brought a nurse. Today was not the shift of that nice girl with the charming smile, but of another nurse, who persisted in saying that it was Dr. I who operated on me.

— I need a shot of something for the pain - I told the nurse.

— What did the doctor tell you? Which one do you want? - she asked.

— Young lady! I don't have a doctor! I haven't seen him once after the operation!

— What do you mean you haven't seen it? - The nurse was surprised.

— That's the way it is! And I don't think I'll ever see him again! - I answered loudly.

— Don't make things up - the nurse said sternly. - What do you mean you won't see him? If he doesn't come to you, there must be a reason for it. Do you know how many seriously ill patients he has? He said that in ten days he himself will take out your stitches!

— Young lady! How else can I tell you to understand? - I spoke irritably. - What stitches? What ten days?! Has your Dr. I. gone completely insane? First of all, I'm tired of lying here for no reason, and in a couple of days I'm going home, and secondly, what is he going to take off my stitches?! My stitches are self-absorbable! I don't have to take them off!

I couldn't have a normal dialogue with the nurse, and I was looking forward to tomorrow and the change of that nice girl with the charming smile.

The husband returned to the room.

— You won't believe it, - he said, looking at me with an indignant look. - Dr. Y. came to the hospital, but he had to leave right away!

— It's okay... - I sighed. - I don't even want to see him anymore. I don't feel well. I'm going to die in this hospital... I have to get out of here. I'll get better sooner at home... I was in the hospital for five days after the first operation last time, and I won't be able to take it any longer now...

Despite my very bad feeling, I tried to get on crutches. I even managed to take a few steps, but after that I lay for a long time absolutely powerless, in a pre-conscious state.

The next day there was a nice girl's shift, and we enjoyed drinking fragrant tea with candy in my room. The nice girl was truly nice. Even when she was at her post, from time to time she still looked into my room, inquired about my well-being and offered her help. It was strange that such an attractive and kind-hearted nurse should be working in this vile place!

In the meantime, our room was becoming full of guests who were going there to smoke and share the latest news.

The thick tobacco smoke enveloped my entire room. The occupants of the "sanctuary" were smoking without fear of being caught, and in a completely relaxed manner. Suddenly, the door of the room opened abruptly:

— What's going on here?! - A man's voice shouted excitedly. Waving his hands, trying to dispel the tobacco smoke, the man in the white coat was extremely astonished by our shameless actions. - What are you doing?! Are you smoking in here?! Have you all lost your minds?! Who let you do this?!

— Yes, - I raised my hand up so that the doctor would turn his attention to me instead of venting his anger on the visitors to my room. - We're smoking in here!

— How dare you?! Who is your doctor?! Answer me! - harshly, even angrily, the man in the white coat addressed me.

— Dr. I.! - I said confidently to the doctor, looking straight into his eyes.

— I'll get him here now! - The emotional and distraught man shook his hands. - And you - he pointed his finger at me - you! - I'll be in trouble! Well, stay with me! And all of you - the doctor pointed at those present - go back to your rooms! - The enraged man in a white coat rushed out the door.

— Do me this favor! I beg of you! Bring me my doctor, at last! - I shouted after me.

There was dead silence in the room for a moment.

— And if he does? - Patient Petya asked me quietly.

— What will happen then?
— Who will he bring? - I asked.
— I don't know... guards, backup...
— Let him do it, - I said firmly. - So I'll fight. I can answer for my behavior and for every word, unlike the nursing staff of this hospital. And I smoke here, by the way, with the permission of the head of the department. He promised me a lot of things while he was hoping to get a so-called "thank you" from me in his office. I have the truth on my side. So I don't think anybody's gonna come in here. Well, if they do, good! It means that not everything in the department is lousy, it means that there are decent people who will hold me accountable! I'm really breaking the law! And besides, my surgeon, he is absolutely real, not imaginary. And I'll be sure to tell him everything, what happened here and what kind of colleagues he has. So, I think one of your doctors - I looked around at those present, - has already explained to this doctor to relax and give up on me. He won't bring anybody! I am glad that our wonderful nurse and nurse's assistant are not with us now. We all will be discharged from here ... and they still have to work in this vile place! - I finished triumphantly.

No one came to the room.

THE MOON IN THE EIGHTH HOUSE

It had been five days since the operation. I didn't feel very well, but I didn't see the point of staying in that hospital anymore. I wanted to go home sooner. At home and the walls help. I called a car to transport the bed-ridden patients, and my husband went to pay for my "treatment" and to get the documents for my discharge. In the end, of course, he brought these documents and they were signed by Dr. I., but they indicated my old, severe and autoimmune diagnosis. It was told to Mr. B. by my surgeon in the very beginning, before I went to this hospital. But at that time my surgeon did not know that I no longer had it.

— What unconscionable people can be - I said as I read my discharge form. - But I brought them all the doctor's reports, all the tests... still they made me a dying person!
— That's right! - My husband supported me. - If they ever get hurt, and no one is immune to that, I wish they'd get to see themselves!
— It was funny, I smiled.
— All right, I don't care about that... let's go home.

It's snowing outside, and the weather is bad. But I'm happy anyway, because I have this amazing, incredible fox vest! Under my tight black skirt and twelve- inch heeled boots, it all looks stunning! What a bliss to be healthy and attractive! I have so much energy right now, I constantly want to move, to do something! Maybe I should write a book? Oh, good idea! I have something to tell the World! :-) My experience can be useful to many people. And besides, I have a huge number of notes... I've been keeping diaries since I was a kid! I'll have to think about it. But afterwards... right now I have to go to Moscow in the evening. I want to play a new jazz CD in my car and take a ride through my favorite places and streets. And life is good! Thank you, Universe, for everything!

My personal diary.
October 2013

THE MOON IN THE EIGHTH HOUSE

THE MOON IN THE EIGHTH HOUSE

REVIEWS

"The Moon in the Eighth House" is a rollicking, cascading, brazen, unashamed, no holds barred celebration of Freaks.

This autobiographical tale bolts at top speed from the get go and shines a bright uncomplaining, brutal, witty, poignant and entertaining light on our author's white knuckle ride through the disability hurly burly years in Russia.

Racing and raging through the 80' s and 90's our author spins a web of celebration, diary entries, anecdotes, and astrological musings to place us squarely into braces and irons.

"I don't settle for anything "average". I am an absolute favorite of Destiny. And everything that it presented to me and will present to me in the future, all unequivocally for the best."

" Over time, having become a good astrologer, I have learned to move within the planets and thereby adjust my destiny a little, maybe even a lot. But a horoscope always aims at its incarnation and everything is bound to manifest in our life, what is written in it…"

From a Westerner's standpoint this is a very useful comparative look at some of the early literature we were obliged to pursue as part of our primary school curriculum.

"I Can Jump Puddles", was an insightful view of childhood in the post-war West with the irons and braces of the polio kind. Of course today polio has somewhat retreated into the distance and Down's, Autism, Cerebral Palsy, spinabif and others now hold sway, and unlike cultural stigmas and bullying attached to the disability,

" Soboleva! You're holding your pen wrong! Hold your pen like the other children!

I was very ashamed of my deformed joints, so I answered her quietly, almost in a whisper:

- I can't do it any other way, my fingers hurt.

But she wouldn't let up:

- Then what are you doing in a school for normal and healthy children?! Go to another school where the sick and retarded study!"

A progressive culture of inclusion now pervades the education system in countries like the U.K. and Australia and thus the reader can appreciate the period, time and cultural differences between Moscow, and the West.

The system is exposed for the cruel bully it is, and the identifying with the "freak show" is brutal and witty by equal measure, and a sophisticate device of befriending pain, in its myriad guises.

The presentation of deformity throughout history and literature is not something that has always sat comfortably with "polite society", but in recent times some probing, confronting and entertaining works have been written inspired by Covid (and odd juxtapositions with Samuel Pepys Diaries), to leprosy, to the hugely successful "Curious Incident of the Dog…" which became an exhilarating piece of theatre.

The Master and Margarita by Bulgacov put ordinary Muscovites into extraordinary situations. In a less magical/ but equally macabre and witty way the good denizens of a modern day Russia must also deal with situations way beyond their comfort zone.

"I was a freak, I wore a leather jacket, and I studied guitar and drums at the

Red Chemist rock lyceum." There is a badge of honour and somewhat turning a perceived negative into a definite positive full of pathos, passion and perverse pain and humour.

Congratulations to Elena Soboleva on a wonderful wily wild yarn.

— Warren Wills,
Producer, composer, theatre director

THE MOON IN THE EIGHTH HOUSE

* * *

"Struggle is a part of life, it's important to use the planets to know how we will struggle."
— *Elena Soboleva*

"*The Moon in the Eighth House*" is a provocative story that is at once feminine, reflecting patient care in post-Soviet Russia, and steeped in personal perseverance prevailing over extraordinary experiences.

The narrator details a life with serious health issues beginning in the Soviet Union in the last century and through the Noughties in modern Russia. She battles difficult problems in an era and area that pose significant challenges. In her youth, she encounters small-minded prejudices and a blanket of mass conformity and cruelty towards the afflicted. By looking to the stars in her study of astrology and reinventing herself through creativity, she reclaims her life and triumphs.

On her journey through the hospitals of Russia, she encounters an eye-popping number of misdiagnoses, severe malpractice, inhumanity, gaslighting and an attempted sexual assault. This is a must read, especially relevant to modern issues in feminism, highlighting how women are not heard by the medical profession and raising a voice against historical abuses of power that resonate in the age of the #MeToo movement.

*— Ola's Kool Kitchen is a DJ,
journalist and editor based in London*

* * *

An incredible woman and a very enjoyable read.

She is a very courageous person.

She takes the reader on her personal journey of pain, self belief and bravery.

The corruption she encountered with no fear of exposing the evil people.

As well as her bravery she also was a skilful business woman using her guile and charm to succeed in a predominate mans world.

I recommend this book.

It will leave you questioning the ethics of those in powerful positions.

Blessings,

*— Bishop Alan Cox OSB
Spiritualist and Radio presenter
www.understandingspirit.com
My facebook pages are "Crystal Radio".
Also "Alan Cox" and "The worldtoheal".*

THE MOON IN THE EIGHTH HOUSE

* * *

Soboleva says she has been described as someone Who can sell any dead car to anyone for any money and this description is pretty much spot on. The Moon In The Eighth House is a collection of memories and experiences packed to the brim with heart and pizazz.

The reader quickly discovers Soboleva is forthright and defiant in the face of her connective tissue autoimmune disorder that could easily have had negatively impacted her life but she calls it a clever girl and attributes it to bringing wonderful men in to her life. The fact she thinks of her illness as having a mind of its own is perhaps a way of separating it from her as a woman.

The theme of astrology and this also being the author's job makes a lot of sense, as her wisdom is very powerful throughout her autobiography. It is very easy to see why people would want her readings and insights about their lives as you do get the sense of a friend speaking to you throughout the book. Her hospital spats are almost farcical but give a sense of the mystical too.

THE MOON IN THE EIGHTH HOUSE

The Moon in the Eighth House is an intense and passionate account of living life to full capacity no matter what life has dealt you and with Elena Soboleva's animated personality that vitality for life will always radiate from every part of her being.

— *Francesca Mepham,
Literature critic*

* * *

When you meet someone whose profession is Astrologer, there is curiosity and scepticism in equal measure. The sceptic in me wants to say 'prove it!' And then my curiosity wants to ask - 'how did you find out?'. This book, graphically, emotionally and frankly tells the story and more than answers my questions. It is a story of a battle to overcome issues that would have broken most people. It is the story of dealing with so called medical professionals more interested in their own worth than their patients and it is the story of relationships and a broken society. Elena has the words and descriptions to engage the reader to side with her, cry with her and will her to overcome her hurdles. At times she tells of an ongoing nightmare which you feel you are part of and want to shout at the characters and at other times she is catches you up in the tenderness of relationships and memories, like an entwined fishing net. The book is an inspiration to humanity and I am grateful for her courage in writing it.

— *Gareth Stamp*
Chairman of the Eurasian Creative Guild

* * *

An incredible book, it's so difficult to set aside until you finish it. The story engrosses you in an emotional whirlpool from the very first lines. It certainly leaves you with a bittersweet aftertaste. Bitter - due to severe episodes of hardship encountered by the author in real life and sweet due to the triumphant outcome achieved by strong determination, perseverance, wit and sometimes sheer luck.

Those who expect a book to tug at your heartstrings – get ready. In vivid terms, you will witness events that will make you cringe; particularly, the 'Soviet' style of mistreatment when people in positions of power, even ordinary school teachers and doctors, take advantage of the unfortunate. At times, you find yourself contemplating that what we take for granted is something that many may be denied. And unfortunately, the most vulnerable among us are the ones who are left to struggle without support and the protection of basic human rights.

The book is also profoundly inspiring and teaches us a valuable lesson to never give up, no matter what. Hope shines through like the North Star in the darkness of the night. And the author demonstrates that even as a child or adolescent, in highly stressful and high-pressure situations, she wasn't mentally and emotionally shattered but survived and thrived. She used her pain and hardship as a building block for a strong character and, subsequently, as a catalyst for accomplishment and success.

It's interesting how she intertwines her life story with astrology and makes us feel that what was destined to happen will happen. You don't choose the circumstances, but you are free to choose your reaction to them. Soboleva skillfully employs simple language for complex life events to motivate you to keep your spirits up and face your fears head-on while wearing your finest attire and a pair of high heels. Can't do it due to a joint ailment? Read and see...

You may shed tears, you may laugh, but without a doubt, you will not be bored.

— *Aizhan Meirambayeva,*
Literature critic

THE MOON IN THE EIGHTH HOUSE

www.ingramcontent.com/pod-product-compliance
Lightning Source LLC
Chambersburg PA
CBHW040319170426
43197CB00022B/2968